CHRISTIAN SERVICES
FOR SCHOOLS

CHRISTIAN SERVICES FOR SCHOOLS

Stuart Thomas

Kevin Mayhew

First published in 1992 by
KEVIN MAYHEW LTD
Rattlesden
Bury St Edmunds
Suffolk IP30 0SZ

ISBN   0 86209 326 0

Front Cover: *The Golden Fish* by Paul Klee (1879-1940).
Kunsthalle, Hamburg/Bridgeman Art Library, London.
Reproduced by kind permission.

Cover design by Graham Johnstone
Typesetting and Page Creation by Anne Haskell
Printed and bound in Great Britain.

Contents

Introduction

As I looked out from my vestry towards the back of the church, my heart sank. Four rows of empty pews on each side of the aisle. Behind that, however, the place had acquired a wall-to-wall covering of parents, grandparents, aunties, friends . . . all eagerly awaiting the grand entrance of the massed pupils and staff of St John's C. of E. (Aided) First School. Yes, it was the school's Christmas service. With an age range from three months (Andrew and David's little sister), to 86 (someone else's Granny). I was supposed to convey meaningfully to all of them the message of Christmas. In addition, there was an expectation that I would enable all of them to enter into the worship; choose carols and songs that everyone knew and loved; cover every personal concern in the building during the prayers; and wish them all a very happy Christmas afterwards, without forgetting anyone's name!

Please don't get me wrong. I'm not against school services – I enjoy them a great deal as it happens – but they do make considerable demands on the time, imagination and energy of whoever leads them. Even three services a year can tax the resources of a busy minister. On the other hand, they provide opportunities unavailable elsewhere. I can't think of any other context where it's possible to communicate the message of the Gospel to so many who would otherwise never darken the doors of a church. Even in the Home Counties Bible Belt, the majority of children rarely, if ever, go to a church service. How many of their parents and other relations would normally be seen in an act of worship? Before our hearts sink into our socks, and the school service becomes another chore to fit into a crowded diary, it's important to consider the potential it offers: not just to create a good impression of the Church; nor even to teach something about the Christian faith; but primarily to provide an environment where people can encounter the living God and be drawn into a relationship with him.

If we are to make the most of the opportunities the school service gives us, our first task is to tune into the various wavelengths present. Everyone in church for that Christmas service came with some kind of agenda, even if not at a conscious level. We need to identify and address those expectations if the aim of service is to be achieved, namely to enable the whole congregation to worship God personally.

THE CHILDREN

Since the service is geared primarily to the children's needs, they should be the main focus. Unlike those regularly attending Sunday services (even Family Services) the children who have been dragged along to the school service are less likely to be familiar with the church environment. Not only is it a different and probably larger building than they are used to, but it's set out quite unlike anywhere else they know. The concept of worship and a liturgy (however informal) will bemuse them if they can't fathom out what's going on. Talking to God, who they can't see, will puzzle those whose parents have never explained to them what prayer is. And because they 'have to go', they'll view the service as a cross between an outing and a glorified assembly! If these thought patterns aren't broken into, concentration will almost certainly take a nosedive, followed immediately by anxiety levels among staff and parents taking off like a rocket. To allow for this, I follow the well-tried KISSES principle – Keep it Safe, Simple, Entertaining and Short.

Keep it safe
There's enough that's strange already, without adding to it! Find out in advance from the staff what the children are learning in RE and assemblies, and build on that. If possible, use hymns and songs they know well – if you don't, there are likely to be embarrassing silences! It's an excellent move to have the children involved in the worship by reading or saying prayers but if they've not had enough time to practise what they've got to say, the service will grind to a halt. The language of Zion may sound impressive, but it goes over a child's head with plenty of room to spare (and most adults would share that experience!). The words and concepts used should be appropriate to the age group and abilities represented, but not patronising – I've never yet encountered a child who takes to being patronised! Children who can't understand what the minister is talking about are rapidly going to find other ways of amusing themselves!

Keep it simple
Complexity isn't a virtue, nor should it be confused with profundity. The theme and structure of the service should be clear to all present. It doesn't matter if the service only lasts for twenty-three minutes, or you haven't explained the meaning of the atonement. Simplicity in every part of the service will enable the children to relate to what's happening and

understand their part in it. Achieving this will take much longer than constructing an intricate web of ideas and themes which tangles them up!

Keep it entertaining
Unfortunately, this is too often equated with 'downmarket' or 'superficial'. Jesus had no fears about entertaining his hearers. The parable of the Great Wedding Feast must have had them in stitches, but this didn't detract from the importance of the message or its underlying seriousness. Used properly the entertainment factor not only holds attention but underlines what's being said. At all costs avoid a string of silly jokes. If it goes over the top the entertainment will overwhelm everything else and turn the service into a pantomime. Quite often the children will have prepared a drama or musical item to perform, which can be built into the overall pattern. It's also essential to engage the minds of those present by involving them, asking questions, using visual aids and even persuading them to do something, as well as watch.

Keep it short
If you let the service go on . . . and on . . . and on . . . you'll cross the boredom threshold and find it impossible to step back again. Excessive length is usually caused by uncertainty about what to say next. Wordiness and worthiness are mutually exclusive. To some extent length can be adjusted according to the age and maturity of the group concerned. Few adults can concentrate for more than ten minutes on one thing, even under good circumstances, and for children that time is much shorter.

Children may not have adult maturity, but they're every bit as capable of entering into worship as any grown-up. Often their simple profundity and perceptiveness will show up the dullness and woolliness of their 'elders and betters'. If those children who might otherwise be drawn towards other activities, are drawn instead to a living faith by services which are attractive, interesting and sincere, they may well become lifelong churchgoers. If their few experiences of church suggest that it's dreary and a waste of time, there's little prospect of them coming back later in life.

The Staff

It is easy to forget the teachers, because they seem just to be doing their job. Teachers will always tell you to plan the service around the children, but they need to be enthused too. If the staff are unenthusiastic, it's highly unlikely that the children will make up for them. Teachers have the unenviable task of keeping order and controlling any riots that break out, so it's no surprise that they look hassled at times. A boring, incomprehensible service makes their life even harder, however, as they try in vain to maintain a vague level of concentration and interest. Too many like that and the school service will be banned! Courtesy demands that the headteacher and at least some staff are consulted about the planning of the service, but they're usually an excellent source of creative ideas and suggestions, too. Co-operation with the staff means that contributions from the children can be planned and practised in advance, and where possible integrated into what's being taught. If the teachers have confidence in the

leader of the service, their anxiety level about the 'performance' will be substantially reduced. The children will also have a much clearer idea of what they're supposed to do, and how their contribution fits into the rest of the service.

The Parents

Most parents experience a lump in their throat when they see their pride and joy taking part in a public event (grandparents can suffer acutely from the same symptom!). I've watched my own daughter often enough in various productions to understand this affliction and realise how difficult it is to focus on anything apart from what she's doing. The parent-child bond is a good and powerful thing, but it does create a distinct ambience when Samantha is chosen to be Mary in the Nativity play, or Jimmy gets landed with reading out a prayer! Sentimentality soon takes over, and the worship easily becomes drowned in the flood of 'Oohs' and 'Aaahs'. The tension level also rises, just in case the offspring have a sudden attack of amnesia, or gets the whole thing wrong. These are things to 'live with', but a well-planned service will help parents especially to feel less wound-up – if the minister is relaxed, it's more likely that others will be, too. Many of them may well not enter a church building for a service unless the school organises it, and if their experience isn't a good one, that will remain the extent of their church-going. Through their children it's quite possible for parents to be drawn closer to God in worship and praise – our job is to provide the right environment.

Establishing Aims and Surmounting Problems

All well and good, but how to achieve this impossible dream? Perfection isn't attainable this side of eternity, but it's astonishing how things can be improved. How often have you said to yourself after a service, 'What was all that about?' Somehow the event didn't quite hang together or convey a sense of purpose. This wasn't due to any lack of sincerity or faith. Probably no-one was clear about the aims of the occasion. It's often said that if you aim at nothing in particular, you'll score a bull's eye.

In one sense all services have the same aim, the worship of God, but that's not really specific enough. Given the particular kind of congregation at a school service, the overriding aim must be twofold – to communicate something of the Christian faith to those who would otherwise not hear it, and to enable them to take part in the worship in a way that enables them to experience the reality of the living God. The mind of the hearers has to be engaged so that they'll receive and understand the message, and their hearts and wills must also be touched by the Holy Spirit if their lives are to change. Every part of the service should be prayerfully considered in the light of the question: 'Will this be a help or a hindrance to understanding and worship?' One theme is therefore plenty, and should be reflected in the hymns, readings and prayers. It's far better to make one good point clearly and well, than to lose three or four in a fog of complexity and uncertainty.

There may be other aims as well, such as attracting more young families into the church, or creating closer links with the school and community. These are admirable but secondary. In fact, if the primary aim is clearly thought out, these others are also more likely to be achieved. Once you know the direction and theme of the service, it's much easier to design it so that the point being made affects both the mind and the heart of the hearer.

Some things, such as the location of the service, may not be negotiable. For the purposes of this book it's assumed that the school will come to church, a state of affairs with many advantages. The children are being taken on a reasonably regular basis to a building they'd otherwise remain unfamiliar with, and will learn that this place is used primarily for worshipping God – very different from the school environment! Hymnbooks and other liturgical facilities will be on hand and the connection between the two institutions is being maintained and reinforced. However, this may present a problem to the teaching staff, who have to organise transport or walk the children, and are removed from their own facilities and resources. Rehearsals may be needed for the 'performers', requiring further transport and time. The building may be cold and uninviting, or even dilapidated, which means that the minister is starting with a built-in disadvantage. A large church will usually mean that all those with a speaking role need to use sound reinforcement in order to be heard properly. Music and musicians need to be carefully placed if they're to lead the singing effectively. None of this is a major difficulty, however, if it's 'planned in'.

The school will probably want to choose the timing of the service to fit in with its own pattern of activity. Many prefer to use the beginning or end of the school day, so that only one journey with the children is needed. This will undoubtedly be more convenient for the majority of parents, who have to deliver or collect their offspring, though it may also mean that the children are either very frisky or rather tired. They'll be most attentive in the middle of the day, but the interests of the staff and parents shouldn't be forgotten.

If the school hall is to be used, the children will be familiar with the surroundings and have everything they need to hand. It isn't quite so easy to create a worshipful atmosphere among the wallbars and fire extinguishers, however. The ideal situation is the school chapel, which combines the advantages of both locations, though in the main these exist only in larger private or public schools. However, there's no perfect environment, and with care most places can be used effectively for worship.

There are plenty of other variables. If the school has a Christian foundation it's likely that the majority of parents and staff will be more sympathetic towards the Christian faith. On the other hand, the school may have a large number of students of other faiths, which creates a different set of problems. Certain schools have a fairly limited age-range, but where this is wider, pitching the service so that all of them feel addressed in some way is vital if some groups are not to feel 'left out'.

The question of inter-faith worship is important, but beyond the scope of this book. Christian ministers are usually asked to conduct Christian services. However much we may regret the difficulties of enabling all the children to worship together, parents who are adherents of other faiths often prefer to remove their children from any activity in which a Christian minister is involved. Accordingly, the assumption of this book is that the worship will be specifically Christian.

The specimen services don't really address the question of style, either, though they can be adapted to most age-groups. As a rough rule of thumb, I work on the principle that beyond the age of eight most children like to think they're nearly adult! However, allowance has to be made for the maturity of thought and behaviour normal for the age-group concerned. It should also be borne in mind that the ability to conceptualise comes relatively late in a child's emotional and mental development. Hymns and songs will also have to suit the age-group you're dealing with, as well as the repertoire they're familiar with. Most ministers develop their own style of leading worship and speaking, and that shouldn't be abandoned just because the context has changed. Rather, it needs to be directed at a particular group and their needs and expectations.

The ideas in this book are ones which have worked for me, but it may well be that in your situation they'll need some adaptation. Although there are suggested hymns and songs, others may be more appropriate to the schools to which you minister. Resources such as this book provides are only a tool to enable us to seize the opportunity of presenting the Good News to those who would otherwise not hear it. However we do it, the responsibility on us is to attract them to God's Church, and, more important still, enable them to enjoy his presence for themselves as a personal reality, both in worship and in their daily lives.

How To Use This Book

Since for the most part there's no fixed liturgy for a school service (except in those schools founded on a particular tradition) the contents of this book are meant to be an aid rather than a strait-jacket. Each section is based on the assumption that hymns, prayers, Bible readings and some kind of address are likely to be included in the majority of acts of worship. Although seasonally structured there are many areas of overlap, and like any resource book, this one should be adapted to your specific situation and needs.

HYMNS

Always a great source of controversy. What you choose will depend in part on the tradition within which you're working, but if possible try to blend old and new. Most children love the livelier modern worship songs, but it's good to encourage them to learn and love hymnody of an earlier generation. The two aren't mutually exclusive, and some of the comments in *In Tune with Heaven* (the Archbishops' Commission report on church music, May 1992) apply to school as well as parish worship. Almost all the hymns suggested here are found either in Hymns Ancient and Modern New Standard, Hymns for Today's Church or Mission Praise, these being among the most popular and easily obtained hymnbooks available today. One or two suggestions only come from the most recent works of Graham Kendrick. I've not included many suggestions for the five-to-seven year-old age group as material varies so greatly between schools. It's best at this stage to consult the staff – many of

their pupils can't read very much, so learning words is essential. In my experience the songs of Ishmael are well-liked by this group.

CONFESSIONS

These may not always be necessary, but acknowledging our wrongdoing is a good habit, not just for its specifically spiritual benefits but because it helps to encourage personal honesty. It may be helpful to introduce confession in such a way that the children understand its purpose within the context of the whole service. Stress too the importance of forgiveness by God, so that a hand-wringing atmosphere is avoided.

PRAYERS

There are vast numbers of prayers for schools in the form of collects, so most of those here are responsive. They can be adapted to any situation by adding biddings or including specific material (at times this is built into them). Where material from other publications has been used this has been acknowledged.

SERMON IDEAS

I've 'road-tested' most of these myself and found them to work. They need a certain amount of patter, and some may not be suited to all ages between five and eighteen. Almost all require some preparation, but the effort is well worth it. Visual reinforcement of a point stays in the mind much longer.

OTHER RESOURCES

Innumerable aids to worship are now available. To pick out a few seems invidious, but one or two stand out as particularly helpful. In general, books such as *Church Family Worship*, *Springboard to Worship*, and *Patterns for*

Worship (difficult to get hold of now) contain plenty of material that could be used in a school service. Seasonal books such as *The Promise of His Glory* and *Lent, Holy Week and Easter* are also worth investigating, though they are primarily aimed at the parish. On the sermon front, *For all the Family* and *More for all the Family* provide plenty of splendid visually based family service sermons which can easily be put to use in a school service. Books of prayers and readings and music are legion, though not all of even quality.

Inevitably with this kind of book you'll find some parts more helpful than others. I'm sure I've omitted someone's favourite hymn or reading! However, I hope its contents will stimulate you to producing a good experience of worship for the school children who come to you: dignified but not stuffy or pompous; serious about the Christian faith but fun; challenging but rewarding.

REFERENCES

Botting M. *For all the Family*. Kingsway Publications, Eastbourne.

The Liturgical Commission (1989) *Patterns for Worship*. Church House Publishing, London.

The Liturgical Commission (1990) *The Promise of His Glory*. Church House Publishing, London.

Perry M. (Ed) (1986) *Church Family Worship*. Hodder & Stoughton, London.

ACKNOWLEDGEMENTS

The publishers wish to express their gratitude to the following for permission to use copyright material:

Church House Publishing, Great Smith Street, London SW1P, for copyright material controlled by the Central Board of Finance of the Church of England from *Patterns for Worship*: A Report of the Liturgical Commission (Church House Publishing 1989).

The Central Board of Finance of the Church of England for extracts from *The Promise of His Glory*: Services and Prayers for the Season from All Saints to Candlemas (Church House Publishing and Mowbray 1991).

Jubilate Hymns, 61 Chessel Avenue, Southampton SO2 4DY, and Hodder & Stoughton for the prayers by Michael Perry from *Church Family Worship*.

The Saint Andrew Press, 121 George Street, Edinburgh EH2 4YN for the prayer from *Worship Now*.

NCEC, Robert Denholm House, Nutfield, Redhill, Surrey RH1 4HW for the prayer *Our Lord Jesus Christ*.

ADVENT & CHRISTMAS

'Christmas comes but once a year' . . . a sentiment to which many of us respond, 'Thank Heavens for that!' 'Too much materialism', some will remark; others complain that 'it's lost all its real meaning'; still more wonder each year 'why do we do it?' Perhaps the biggest single factor in most people's experience of Christmas is the sheer slog of buying presents ('whatever can we get Uncle Bill this year?'), sending cards ('we'll never hear the last of it if we don't send her one') and the pressure of getting it all done by the great day ('they'll have sold out by Saturday, so we've got to go now'). The Christmas run-up is so long that we need two bank holidays to recover!

From a Christian viewpoint we easily miss out on Advent in all this frantic hyperactivity. Instead of enjoying one of the richest seasons of the Church's year, we get spiritual indigestion from non-stop carols and recitations of Luke 2. This is made more complex in the case of schools because not only do they break up well before Christmas itself (half-way through Advent in some private schools), but they also expect a full Christmas service. Somehow, the children are perceived to be missing out if they don't get 'the full works'. For a Christian minister with a number of schools under his pastoral wing, this is a trial of both strength and imagination. Just to add to the problem, it's impossible to use the same material two years' running!

At a recent conference on worship between Advent and Candlemas, one of the speakers was clearly heard to say that most clergy hold out against carols until the third Sunday in Advent. After that they have to accept the inexorable flow and go with it. Perhaps ministers just have to sing too many Christmas hymns, but there are times when all of us have wished the herald angels would stop singing for a bit, or that the faithful would come rather less frequently. Is there a way round this problem? With due thought, there's no reason why a perfectly acceptable Christmas service shouldn't include less familiar material. A clear theme running through the service (such as 'The Light of the World' or 'The Word made Flesh') should suggest a wider range of hymns and readings. It's completely in order for the minister to establish this with the staff well in advance. If the school are coming into the church, they would normally expect to allow the minister to have some say in the content of the worship. Many schools would probably welcome an Advent Service of some kind, at least as a refreshing alternative, and if some Christmas carols are mandatory, why not devise a service which covers both Advent and Christmas? There is some excellent modern material available, well within the scope of most children aged seven or over, and this too can help to lighten the texture of the liturgy. At any time of year it's a good move to let children do readings or prayers, but there may also be scope for a carol competition, perhaps in conjunction with the church choir. At all costs we should avoid bawling out carols for their own sake. If those present are to be drawn into worshipping God, they'll respond to an attractive, thoughtful service, not a knees-up.

Advent Sunday

One of the great themes of Advent is light. Its symbolism is rich and powerful and can be used in many ways. Sharing the light is invariably a moving and profound experience for the congregation, though its impact is best in the late afternoon or evening. Even a small number of candles produce a remarkable amount of light, so don't be afraid to switch off or dim the main lights.

SHARING THE LIGHT

Each member of the congregation is given a candle, preferably with a drip-shield. If the building's large enough, gather all the congregation at the rear, except for one, who stands by a previously lighted candle at the opposite end. If this isn't possible, form a group of representative members (e.g. of year groups, parents, staff or visitors) who stand at the back while the rest of the congregation remain standing in their pews. As some quiet music is played, the person by the candle lights their own and walks down to share the light with those at the back. They all then return to their places to share the light with the rest of the congregation. A choir singing 'Thou whose almighty Word' very softly creates just the right atmosphere, but an organ, instrumental group or even a recording will also provide a suitable background. The sight of the light growing as it's passed on from one to another is an effective picture of the spread of the Good News, until the whole world is filled with the light of Jesus.

HYMNS

Traditional

Thou whose almighty Word
Lo! He comes
O come, O come Emmanuel
Christ is the world's light
Hark the glad sound
Hark! A thrilling voice
Hills of the north rejoice
Hail to the Lord's anointed
Come, thou long-expected Jesus
Thy Kingdom come

Modern

The earth was dark
Darkness like a shroud
From Heaven you came
Like a candle flame
The light of Christ
When he comes
Make way, make way
Light has dawned
Lift up your heads
Shine Jesus, shine

READINGS

Genesis 1:1-5/Isaiah 2:1-5/Jeremiah 33:14-16/Zechariah 8:3-8/
1 Corinthians 1:3-9/1 Thessalonians 5:4-9/Revelation 21:22-22:5/
Matthew 25:1-13/Mark 13:32-end/
Luke 21:29-36/John 9:1-11.

CONFESSION

Lord Jesus, you are the Light of the World, who reveals to us the darkness of our sin and failure. We acknowledge the wrong which spoils our relationship with you; uncaring actions, unkind words and selfish attitudes. We are truly sorry, and ask for your forgiveness. As we open our hearts to you, fill us with your glorious light, that in our lives others may see you shining through. Amen.

Almighty God, who is always more ready to forgive than we are to repent, forgive all your sins, restore you to the light of his presence, and fill you anew with his Holy Spirit, through Christ our Lord. Amen.

PRAYER

We come before Christ our Saviour
with our prayers, saying,
Jesus, Light of the world,
Shine in the darkness, we pray.

We pray for all those who suffer
through homelessness, unemployment
or poverty . . .
Help them to know that in you
they have riches, purpose and
an eternal home.
Jesus, Light of the World,
Shine in the darkness, we pray.

We pray for all who live with failure
and distress . . .
Help them to know the victory
of your Cross.
Jesus, Light of the World,
Shine in the darkness, we pray.

We pray for all who are friendless,
lonely and in despair . . .
Help them to find in you
the faithful friend, who will
always stay beside them.
Jesus, Light of the World,
Shine in the darkness, we pray.

We pray for all who are ill in mind or
body . . .
Help them to feel your healing touch
on their lives.
Jesus, Light of the World,
Shine in the darkness, we pray.

We pray for those who rule our
country and our world . . .

Help them to show your compassion to
all who are helpless and vulnerable.
Jesus, Light of the World,
Shine in the darkness, we pray.

We pray for ourselves, that we may
share the light of your presence with
everyone we meet . . .
Help us to draw others to you,
the one true light.
Jesus, Light of the World,
**Shine in the darkness, we pray, and
reveal your glory throughout the
world. Amen.**

SERMON IDEA

Ideally the church should be in near darkness for this (though total darkness may make some feel 'creepy'). If candles are in use ask the congregation to blow them out (they may be more than ready to do so by this stage!), but keep one alight. You'll need one volunteer, and if you aren't using candles you'll also need a small torch. Since the service is about Jesus, the Light of the World, you can encourage the congregation to think about the effect and impact of light, and demonstrate how Jesus can do the same in our own lives.

1 Light gets rid of darkness wherever it is. This can be shown easily with the torch or candle (though take care the latter doesn't blow out). Jesus came to take away the darkness from people's lives – he healed the blind, the sick and the handicapped and released them into a new kind of living. Above all he dealt with sin, which brings darkness into all our lives. As we allow Jesus' light to shine into our lives we'll find he drives away the

dark areas, such as fear, anger and resentment.

2   Light shows us what needs to be done. Arrange for a small, well-situated pile of junk to be placed where the light can fall on it. In the darkness we can't see the rubbish, and might trip over it, but the light shows we need to deal with it. Jesus shows us the things in our own lives which need to be dealt with, and by confessing our sins we allow him to start removing the debris which will otherwise burden us and cause us harm.

3   Light shows us the way to go. In the dark we grope around, afraid to move about because we might bump into things or fall and injure ourselves. Even if we remain uninjured we haven't a clue where to go. Only with a light before us can we walk confidently. Jesus doesn't just come to 'sort us out'. He wants us to walk with him in the light, trusting him to take us in the right direction. Just as light is always there, so Jesus is always with us, forgiving us, helping us and guiding us.

Bible Sunday – The Prophets

The second Sunday in Advent is traditionally 'Bible Sunday', when we thank God for his written word. The new lectionary in 'The Promise of His Glory' stresses the role of the prophets. These two themes overlap and complement each other well. The trap to avoid is 'Bibliolatry' – the worship of the written word of God rather than the Living Word. The prophets were pointing towards Jesus the Messiah, as does the whole of Scripture. It may be helpful during the first hymn to have a child bring up a copy of the Bible (large enough for all to recognise) and lay it on the altar, or well-placed table.

HYMNS

Traditional

Hark, the glad sound
Father of mercies
Lord, I have made thy word my choice
Help us, O Lord, to learn
Thou whose almighty Word
Lord, thy word abideth
How firm a foundation
O Word of God incarnate

Modern

Long ago, prophets knew
Jesus, name above all names
You are the King of Glory
Seek ye first
These are the facts
O what a mystery I see
Spirit of God, unseen as the wind
Wonderful Counsellor

READINGS

Isaiah 11:1-10/40:1-5/55:6-11/Romans 15:1-6/2 Timothy 3:4-4:5/Hebrews 4:12-13/Mark 1:1-8/Luke 4:14-22/ John 5:36-47.

CONFESSION

Lord God, we have disobeyed your laws, and not heeded your word. We have not walked in your ways or allowed you to direct our hearts. We repent of our sinfulness, and humbly ask for your forgiveness. Take away all that spoils our lives, and restore us to yourself. May your word be a lamp for our feet and a light to our path, through Christ our Lord. Amen .

PRAYER

As we read his word, let us pray to God for strength to live as he has commanded us, saying,
Father in Heaven,
Help us to obey.

When we feel angry and resentful, or tempted to speak in unkind and hurtful ways,
Father in Heaven,
Help us to obey.

When we feel anxious or afraid, and do not trust you to keep us in your loving care,
Father in Heaven,
Help us to obey.

When we feel ill or distressed, and do not experience the joy of your presence in our lives,
Father in Heaven,
Help us to obey.

When we feel weak and helpless, and everything seems beyond our strength or ability,
Father in Heaven,
Help us to obey.

When we feel tempted to do things in our own strength, following our own wisdom rather than your commands, Father in Heaven,

Help us to obey. Speak to our hearts through your word, and help us to live by what it says, through Jesus Christ our Lord. Amen.

SERMON IDEAS

1 If you follow the theme of 'prophets', you could use a newspaper to demonstrate differing aspects of the prophet's role. The weather forecast is a good way to start. Encourage people to guess at what the weather will be like in three days' time, then explain that with the help of barometers, computers, satellites and other aids, the weathermen can predict far more accurately what will happen. A sports report on a forthcoming match or event might come next. In this case, no-one can be certain, but for example, Liverpool, are very likely to beat Torquay at football (substitute whatever teams are most likely to get a response). Then move on to current affairs, particularly uncertain situations. Here you should explain that even those who are experts find it difficult to be clear about what might happen. In parallel with all this, show how the prophets at times spoke of what was happening or about to happen: sometimes about what would happen if God's people refused to obey him; and at other times about future events which were as yet unclear. In all of this they were pointing towards Christ, who was the ultimate fulfilment of the whole of the Old Testament. To involve the children, get them to read out suitable headlines or paragraphs.

2 If you take the track of 'God's word', you could use words as a powerful example:

a) God's word warns us (hold up a suitable warning sign and explain that the Bible contains many warnings about what the consequences of wrong behaviour or attitudes will be.)

b) God's word informs us (display an encyclopaedia which contains facts, but stress that the Bible does far more than just give us knowledge – it also tells us how to apply that knowledge in our lives).

c) God's word encourages us (take a familiar advertising slogan and show how we're being encouraged to buy that product – however, God's word isn't a sales pitch, and through it his Holy Spirit persuades us of its truth, and that we need to act upon that truth.)

John The Baptist

John the Baptist doesn't sit easily in a twentieth century context. He was by any standards an odd figure in his own generation; in ours, which isn't used to the prophetic tradition, he can seem quite irrelevant. However, he does follow on naturally from the prophets in Advent (Second Sunday) and points us towards the imminent coming of Jesus. He stands at the crossroads of the Old and New Covenants, and from him we learn about repentance and 'amendment of life'.

HYMNS

Traditional

On Jordan's bank
Lo! In the wilderness a voice
Hark, a thrilling voice
Rejoice, the Lord is King
Awake, awake, fling off the night
Hark, the glad sound
Christ, whose glory
Lo, he comes
The Lord will come
Fill thou my life

Modern

Who can sound the depths of sorrow
Lord have mercy on us
Restore, O Lord, the honour
    of your name
River, wash over me
O Lord, the clouds are gathering
Reign in me
He has showed you
From the sun's rising
Jesus, you are changing me
For this purpose

READINGS

Isaiah 35/49:8-13/Amos 8:1-6/Malachi 3:1-5/4:1-6 Corinthians 4:1-5/James 5:7-10/1 Peter 1:3-12/Matthew 11:2-11/Luke 3:1-20/John 1:6-8, 19-34.

CONFESSION

Loving Father, you sent your servant John the Baptist to prepare the way for the coming of our Saviour Jesus Christ. He called your people to repent of their disobedience and follow the paths of truth and righteousness. As we hear that same call, may our hearts be directed towards your commands, and our wills to the service of your eternal kingdom, through Jesus Christ our Lord, Amen.

PRAYER

We bring to our heavenly Father
the needs of the world around us,
saying:
Father, take our lives,
And make us ready for your coming.

We bring before you all who declare your love and proclaim your good news in the face of apathy, opposition, hatred or violence. May we follow their example of courage and commitment to the Gospel.
Father, take our lives,
And make us ready for your coming.

We bring before you all who suffer because of their Christian faith and willingness to uphold the standards of your Kingdom. May we share their righteousness and integrity.
Father, take our lives,
And make us ready for your coming.

We bring before you all who seek to apply the teaching of the Gospel to their daily work. May we in our tasks and responsibilities bring the light of Christ to those in darkness.
Father, take our lives,
And make us ready for your coming.

We bring before you the leaders of our country and our world, as their policies and decisions affect the lives of all who dwell on this earth. May we act wisely and carefully, for the good of all mankind.

Father, take our lives,
And make us ready for your coming.

We bring before you all who suffer through ill-health, depression, fear, loneliness and bereavement. May we share their burdens and play our part in meeting their needs.

Father, take our lives,
And make us ready for your coming.
Fill our hearts with your love as we
proclaim your word in the world,
through Christ our Lord. Amen.

Sermon Idea

Since John the Baptist prepared the Lord's way, 'being ready' is a good theme to work on.

1 Bring on a previously briefed volunteer, who should be dressed as tattily as possible (gardening clothes or similar will do). Explain that they're on their way to meet the Queen. Since you're likely to get some kind of response to this, ask what's wrong. Develop this into a discussion of how we make ourselves properly ready to meet someone. We prepare to meet with God, not by wearing special clothes, but by getting rid of all the things that make us too unclean to come into his presence as King of Kings. Repentance and forgiveness make this possible.

2 Bring on a second actor, wearing a long dressing gown and lounging around. This time, say the person is ready for school. Since this too will elicit some response, point out that to be ready to go to school we must be properly dressed (remove the dressing gown to reveal full school uniform). To be ready to go places for God we must wear suitable 'clothes' – kindness, unselfishness, patience, etc.

3 Finally, bring on someone in sporting gear. Explain that this one really is ready for action. Cricket kit is good, though football strip will also work, so long as a football is held by the player. Point out that God by his Holy Spirit equips us to do the things he has commanded us.

Mary

In comparison with John the Baptist, Mary seems positively normal. An ordinary young girl, just starting to get excited about her wedding to a very ordinary man. In fact, Jesus' birth is remarkable only because it's so unremarkable. There's no evidence to suggest he was born into real poverty, though his family home certainly wouldn't have had many of the trappings of wealth. Mary speaks to us of trust and obedience (the latter needs careful handling with schoolchildren if they're not immediately to switch off). It's important not to associate Christian obedience with blind adherence to a code of conduct. Obeying God isn't like keeping to the school rules. Rather, we obey God's will out of love for him, and because we put our faith in him.

HYMNS

Traditional

Come, thou long-expected Jesus
For Mary, mother of our Lord
O come, O come Emmanuel
To the name of our salvation
Thy Kingdom come, on bended knee
Love divine, all loves excelling
Tell out, my soul
God is working his purpose out
Thou didst leave thy throne

Modern

My soul doth magnify the Lord
Emmanuel, Emmanuel
Fear not, rejoice and be glad
Light has dawned
I want to walk with Jesus Christ
Seek ye first the Kingdom of God
Let it be to me
Like a candle flame
Lord Jesus Christ

READINGS

Isaiah 7:10-14/11:1-9/42:1-12/Micah 5:1-4/Hebrews 1:1-9/Romans 1:1-7/Matthew 1:18-end/Luke 1:26-38/39-45.

CONFESSION

Eternal God, you called the Virgin Mary to obey your will and trust your promises. We acknowledge our failures and self-will, asking you to forgive us for going our own way rather than putting our faith in your word. Increase our confidence in your leading, and grant us the strength to follow your ways, through Jesus Christ our Lord. Amen.

Almighty God, who forgives all who turn to him in repentance, have mercy on you, deliver you from the path which leads to destruction, and increase in you the will to walk in his ways, through Jesus Christ our Lord. Amen.

PRAYER

Let us pray to the Lord who calls us, saying,
Your Kingdom come,
Your will be done.

You sent your Son into this world to share our humanity and become one of us. May we hear your call to share the lives of others and find you in them. Father in Heaven,
your Kingdom come,
Your will be done.

You sent your Son to teach us the ways of your Kingdom. May we hear your call to proclaim the good news and joyfully fulfil the great commission. Father in Heaven,
your Kingdom come,
Your will be done.

You sent your Son to suffer shame and humiliation for our sake, and to give his life as a ransom for many.
May we hear your call, counting it gain to suffer loss, and give up our lives for his sake.
Father in Heaven,
your Kingdom come,
Your will be done.

You raised your Son from the grip of death, defeating all the powers of sin and evil for ever. May we hear your call to share his victory and live his risen life.
Father in Heaven,
your Kingdom come,
Your will be done, until the whole earth lives to praise your holy name. Amen.

SERMON IDEA
An overhead projector (OHP) or flipchart will be a great help in this sermon. The aim is to demonstrate from Mary's life what obedience to God involves. A separate acetate sheet or flipchart sheet will be needed for each heading, plus a suitable drawing.

1 Mary *listened* to God. We can't obey anyone unless we first hear what it is they want us to do. If we don't listen to the teacher telling us what homework to do (adjust this for younger age-groups) we'll get it wrong. A picture of an ear will do, or of someone listening carefully.

2 Mary *accepted* what God said. That wasn't easy for her, and made her life very complicated. But she knew God was in control, that his plan was the best. Obedience sometimes involves doing something we don't like or find hard (a drawing of someone having difficulty doing something, e.g. almost falling off a bike) but God promises to give us strength to do whatever he commands.

3 Mary *remembered* what God said. We tend to forget what he says to us, because we're so easily distracted by other things (a picture of a few people having fun, but ignoring a cross a little way off).

4 Mary *did* what God said. Obedience ultimately is about doing what we're told. It cost Mary a great deal to go God's way, but she did so willingly and without complaint, because she recognised that by so doing, God's perfect will for mankind would be accomplished. A picture of Mary kneeling before the cross would complement this well.

Christingle

Christingle services are now so widespread that they've almost become a fixed part of the Christmas scene. Although they originated in Moravia in the fourteenth century, most people now associate them with the Children's Society, who restarted them in their modern form in the late sixties. The Christingle is an orange, which symbolises the world, with a candle pushed into the top to represent Jesus the Light of the World. Around it is a red ribbon representing the blood of Christ which was shed for the whole world; and four cocktail sticks with small sweets or dried fruit on them, to stand for the fruits of the earth. The Christingle is a powerful visual aid in its own right, so it's important not to let it be taken over by anything else. It isn't difficult to make, and could be a useful way of involving children or parents, though don't forget to allow enough time.

Like the Advent Sharing of Light service, the Christingle service makes its greatest impact when the day is nearly done. When everyone has given in their gift and collected a Christingle, the lights are switched off and carols sung by candlelight. With adult supervision even small children can do this safely. The Children's Society produce a pack of material and instructions every year and they should be informed of the date and time of your planned service. Their pack also includes various liturgical materials. It's worth emphasising the giving as well as the receiving, since the latter is usually uppermost in children's minds at Christmas.

Christingle services are suitable for any time between Advent and Epiphany, and have great flexibility. They're especially good for younger children, but shouldn't become marginalised to that age-group.

HYMNS

Traditional
Be thou my vision
Christ,whose glory fills the skies
Brightest and best
Christ is the world's light
Join all the glorious names
Jesus shall reign
The race that long in darkness pined
Mine eyes have seen the glory

Modern
The Light of Christ
God whose love (Christingle hymn)
All earth was dark
The Spirit lives to set us free
O Lord, all the world belongs to you
How lovely on the mountains
Like a candle flame
Light has dawned

In addition to these, suitable carols can be sung if Christmas is near enough.

READINGS

Isaiah 9:2,6,7 / 60:1-3 / Colossians 3:1-4 / 1 Thessalonians 5:4-11 / Revelation 1:12-16 / Luke 2:8-14 / Matthew 5:14-16 / John 9:1-11.

CONFESSION

Lord of Truth, your light shines in our hearts, showing up all that is unworthy of your love. We confess that we do not deserve to come into your presence as your children. Forgive us for rejecting your ways and draw us back to yourself, that we may see your glory and be cleansed from all our sins, for the sake of your Son, Jesus Christ our Saviour. Amen.

Almighty God,who has mercy on all who acknowledge their sins, grant unto you forgiveness, peace and the light of his presence, now and for ever. Amen.

PRAYER

Gracious God, we give you thanks and praise for Jesus Christ our Lord;
for he was the word before all creation.
Through him all things come to be;
not one thing has its being but through him.
Jesus, light of the world,
We worship and adore you.

Your life is the light that shines in the dark, a light that darkness cannot overpower.
Jesus, light of the world,
We worship and adore you.

The Word was the true light coming into the world. You were in the world, that had its being through you, and the world did not know you.
Jesus, light of the world,
We worship and adore you.

You came to your own, and they did not accept you. But to all who accept you, you give power to become children of God.
Jesus, light of the world.
We worship and adore you.

The Word was made flesh and lived among us, and we have seen his glory, as the only Son of the Father, full of grace and truth.
Jesus, light of the world,
We worship and adore you.

To God our creator, born as one of us, be all praise and glory.
With all the company of heaven, we worship you, saying,
Holy, holy, holy is the Lord God almighty,
who was, and is, and is to come;
to him be glory and honour for ever and ever. Amen.

From *The Promise of His Glory*

SERMON IDEA

Take a shoe box, or a similar-sized carton, and completely line the interior with black paper or card. On small sheets of paper write down various forms of 'darkness' to be found in our world. These can be varied according to the age-group. With under-twelves I wrote a sentence, e.g. 'I'm lonely', which a child then read out. After a brief explanation I then gave Jesus' reply, e.g. 'With me you'll always find a faithful friend'. Other sentences could include, 'I'm afraid', 'I'm hopeless', 'I'm useless', 'I'm too bad' or 'I'm too busy'.

With older children and teenagers you could write 'no friends', 'no job', 'no money', 'no hope', etc. No more than seven slips of paper should be put into the box, to be drawn out one at a time. You'll need the 'replies' written out separately, where you can see them; if possible, commit them to memory. Ideally the 'darknesses' you choose should be a combination of physical and spiritual, to avoid an unhelpful dualism. The replies are best based on words of Jesus himself.

A Gift Service

We live in such a materialistic environment that thinking of others at Christmas time can be quite a strain. The idea of a service at which children bring forward gifts for those who would not otherwise receive any, is one used in many churches. It transfers quite well to the school setting. One way to develop this is to persuade the children to work and earn money with which to buy a suitable present; £1 for a week's washing up, and £1 for cleaning the car soon builds up to sufficient for a gift. The tasks clearly have to be appropriate to the age group. There's always a tendency for this exercise to be regarded as 'conscience money' – a way of damping down guilt feelings about the cost of our personal celebrations of Christmas. Instead, try to emphasise God's gifts to us, supremely the gift of his Son. We can only give back to him what he's already given us; as we offer him what we can, he takes it and uses it for his Kingdom. Emphasis should be on giving as a joy, not a chore or regrettable duty. The service needs a point where wrapped gifts can be brought forward, but first ensure there's a good outlet for all this generosity. No organisation wants more presents than it can actually give away. It's also a good idea to set a limit to the cost of a gift (say £4). If there isn't a top limit those who can afford less may end up being embarrassed by larger presents from others. This service really needs to take place early enough to enable the gifts to be distributed before Christmas.

HYMNS
Traditional
Take my life and let it be
Praise God from whom
Thou who wast rich

Amazing Grace
Teach me, my God and King
For the fruits of his creation
Lord of all power
In the bleak midwinter

Modern
At this time of giving
O what a gift
The Lord has led forth his people
I want to walk with Jesus Christ
Give me joy in my heart
Let us talents and tongues
Father, we adore you
Holy Child

READINGS
1 Chronicles 29:6-14/Malachi 3:6-12
2 Corinthians 8:8-15/9:6-15
James 1:12-18/1 Peter 4:7-11/Matthew 5:11-16 Luke 18:18-30/21:1-4.

CONFESSION
We come before God who has given us everything, confessing our selfishness and greed, saying,
Father, forgive us,
And create a right spirit within us.

For keeping our possessions to ourselves, and refusing to share them with those in need,
Father, forgive us,
And create a right spirit within us.

For doing what we want to, but not allowing others to make claims on our time,
Father, forgive us,
And create a right spirit within us.

For losing our temper and being unkind, instead of showing others patience and sensitivity,

Father, forgive us,
And create a right spirit within us.

For trying to preserve our image
instead of giving ourselves to the
service of others,
Father, forgive us,
And create a right spirit within us.
Cleanse us from self-centredness and
fill our hearts with the love of Christ,
who gave his life that we might live,
Amen.

PRAYER

We bring before God the needs
of our world, saying,
Loving Father,
Give your peace.

We pray for your church throughout
the world . . . As your people serve you,
Loving father,
Give your strength.

We pray for your world, and all who
are entrusted with the responsibility of
governing it . . . As they make
decisions which shape our lives,
Loving Father,
Give your courage.

We pray for our families and
friends . . . As we live together,
Loving Father
Give your love.

We pray for all who suffer or are in
need . . . As they face their problems
and sadnesses,
Loving Father,
Give your healing.

We pray for ourselves . . . As we
worship and work together,

Loving Father,
Give your joy. May we offer ourselves
gladly to your service, and willingly
follow your example of self-giving,
through Jesus Christ our Lord. Amen.

SERMON IDEA

There are many kinds of gifts, and by
highlighting some of them you can
make various points about God's gifts
to us, and our giving to him. For
example, there are 'earned gifts' – not
so much gifts as a reward for services
rendered. Explain that God doesn't
give us anything because we deserve it,
but simply because he loves us.
Similarly, we give to God because we
love him. Then there are unexpected
gifts, which take us by surprise,
showing that someone cares about us
or remembers us. God's gifts are a sign
of his unending care for us. There are
useful gifts, and God gives us gifts to
be used in his service. Then there are
love gifts, like a red rose. They aren't
earned or even useful, just a token of
love. Explain how all these categories
are covered by God's gift to us of his
Son.

A Crib Service

Crib Services are awkward to organise in a school context. The possibility of building up to Christmas Day, when the infant Jesus is placed in the crib, isn't there, and few schools are open on Christmas Eve. However, for the younger age-group the symbolism is effective, and the cumulative effect can be generated through the service. Some will have reservations about blessing any inanimate object not to be used sacramentally, but it's still possible to use the crib scene as a 'model' which points us to the reality of the Incarnation. If possible, use a crib with as many movable parts as you can. This gives the address much more flexibility.

HYMNS

Traditional
Once in Royal David's City
Away in a manger
O little town of Bethlehem
In the bleak mid-winter
Silent Night
What child is this
Child in the manger
While shepherds watched
Sing Lullaby
Little Jesus

Modern
See him a-lying on a bed of straw
Holy Child
This Child
Like a Candle Flame
From Heaven you came
Come and join the celebration
Little Donkey
Joy to the World
Look to the skies
Emmanuel, Emmanuel

READINGS

Isaiah 9:6-7 / Titus 3:4-7 / Matthew 1:18-25 / Luke 2:1-7 (or 15).

CONFESSION

Heavenly Father, you sent your Son into our world to live as one of us and die for all of us. We are sorry that we haven't recognised your coming into our lives or allowed your glory to fill our hearts with praise. Grant us the trust of Mary, the joy of the shepherds and the generosity of the wise men, and willingness to share the Good News of Christmas with all around us. Amen.

PRAYER

Let us worship the Saviour. Heavenly King, yet born of Mary;
Jesus, Son of God,
We praise and adore you.

Eternal Word, yet child without speech;
Jesus, Son of God,
We praise and adore you.

Robed in glory, yet wrapped in infant clothes;
Jesus, Son of God,
We praise and adore you.

Lord of Heaven and earth,
yet laid in a manger;
Jesus, Son of God,
We praise and adore you.

To you, O Jesus,
strong in your weakness,
glorious in your humility,
mighty to save,
be all praise and glory,
with the father and the Holy Spirit,
now and for ever. Amen.

From *Worship Now*

Sermon Idea

The crib is the central visual aid, so anything else used must complement its symbolism. Display a model train or car, preferably one with a fair amount of detail that looks realistic. Point out that like the real thing it can move forwards and backwards, but that it does have some deficiencies (e.g. it can't take passengers, though in the case of a train, it might reach its destination a bit more quickly!).

The model is more than just a reminder – as we play with it we can get an idea of the real thing – but it's no substitute. Then bring out a doll, also fairly realistic. Explain that small children can have a real 'relationship' with a doll, but as they get older they mustn't let this become a substitute for relationships with human beings. In the same way the crib isn't a substitute for the real thing. Like a toy, it is put away until it's next used, whereas the reality is always there. As we look at it we get an idea of what that first Christmas was like, but the truth of the Christian faith is that the incarnation was only the beginning of the story.

We grow up recognising that models may give us fun, and help us understand what they represent in a basic way, but that the real thing is far more important and rewarding. Similarly, as we grow in faith we see the crib and thank God that through Jesus and our relationship with him we can experience the reality of God in a far deeper way.

The Christmas Service

With the possible exception of services celebrating the foundation of a school, no service is more overlaid with expectations than 'the Christmas Service'. Since almost everyone will want to sing carols and hear the Christmas story, the pattern of 'nine lessons and carols' can be ideal (if rather too long for smaller children). The King's College Cambridge sequence of readings isn't statutory, even if tradition has given that liturgy an authority almost equal to that of Scripture! Some suggestions, based on material found in The Promise of His Glory *are included below. It's most important to ensure that the carols chosen reflect the readings (likewise any choral items). A sermon may be out of place, but an idea is included for situations that could benefit from it. Some schools will put more emphasis on tradition than others, but whatever the approach, you should ensure that the Christmas story is set in the context of the whole Gospel, and that it comes across as the culmination of God's activity in the Old Testament and the focal point of our salvation.*

HYMNS AND READINGS

Set 1

Reading	Micah 5:2-4
Hymn	O little town of Bethlehem
Reading	Haggai 2:5b-9
Hymn	A great and mighty wonder
Reading	Isaiah 11:1-9
Hymn	It came upon the midnight clear
Reading	Luke 12:35-40
Hymn	When he comes
Reading	Luke 1:26-38
Hymn	O, what a mystery I see
Reading	Philippians 2:5-11
Hymn	From Heaven you came
Reading	Luke 2:1-14 (or 20)
Hymn	Angels from the realms

Set 2

Reading	Ezekiel 34:11-15
Hymn	While shepherds watched
Reading	Jeremiah 22:13-16/23:5-6
Hymn	The light of Christ
Reading	Isaiah 40:1-11
Hymn	Ding dong! Merrily on high
Reading	John 10:11-18
Hymn	Once in royal David's city
Reading	Luke 1:46-55
Hymn	Tell out my soul
Reading	Titus 2:11-14
Hymn	Look to the skies
Reading	Matthew 1:18-end
Hymn	Of the Father's love begotten

Set 3

Reading	Genesis 1:1-5
Hymn	In the bleak midwinter
Reading	Zechariah 2:10-13
Hymn	Lord Jesus Christ
Reading	Isaiah 9:2/6-7
Hymn	Unto us a boy is born
Reading	Luke 2:1-14
Hymn	On Christmas night
Reading	Romans 1:1-6
Hymn	Long ago, prophets knew
Reading	Hebrews 1:1-9
Hymn	See amid the winter's snow
Reading	John 1:1-14
Hymn	Hark! The herald angels sing

CONFESSION

Lord of grace and truth, we confess our unworthiness to stand in your presence as your children.
We have sinned;
Forgive – and heal us.

The Virgin Mary accepted your call to be the mother of Jesus. Forgive our disobedience to your will.
We have sinned;
Forgive – and heal us.

Your Son, our Saviour, was born in poverty in a manger. Forgive our greed and rejection of your ways.
We have sinned;
Forgive – and heal us.

The shepherds left their flocks to go to Bethlehem. Forgive our self-interest and lack of vision.
We have sinned;
Forgive – and heal us.

The wise men followed the star to find Jesus the King. Forgive our reluctance to seek you.
We have sinned;
Forgive – and heal us.

May the God of all healing and forgiveness draw you to himself, that you may behold the glory of his Son, the Word made flesh, and be cleansed from all your sins through Jesus Christ our Lord. **Amen.**

From *Patterns for Worship*

PRAYER
As we come into the presence of the Christ child, we bring our prayers through him to our Heavenly Father, saying,
Eternal Word,
Be born in us today.

We pray, Father God, for all who are celebrating the birth of your Son with us this Christmas time. We ask that, with them, we may be joyful witnesses to your saving love.

Eternal Word,
Be born in us today.

We pray, Father God, for all whose experience of Christmas will be dark, lonely or sad. We ask that we may bring them the comfort of your presence and the joy of your unending love.
Eternal Word,
Be born in us today.

We pray, Father God, for all those whose Christmas will be wrecked by hatred, tension or violence. We ask that the peace your Son came to bring may reign in the hearts of men and women throughout the world.
Eternal Word,
Be born in us today.

We pray, Father God, for all whom we love, all who share our life in the school, family or the community. We ask that the love of Christ may be seen in all our relationships one with another.
Eternal Word,
Be born in us today.

We pray, Father God, that your Son will be at the heart of our celebrations today, and our lives for evermore.
Eternal Word,
Be born in us today, and bring us to share in your unending life. Amen.

SERMON IDEA
This can't be used too often. It has impact if only a few people, other than the participants, know what is going to happen – but it's recommended that you warn the Headteacher beforehand. You need to be quite sure you can control the chaos. Two readers come up and start to read the Christmas story

from Luke's gospel (you can say that no-one was listening earlier). As they start reading, others come up with the Radio Times, a bottle of sherry, crackers, oranges, a fairy, tinsel, decorations . . . anything which covers up the message of Christmas. Ideally a few noisy secular songs will also drown out the reading. The point is obvious – all these other things can stop us hearing and seeing the reality of Christmas. When all the items are up, call for total silence. Try not to explain this too much. The point is so powerful that little else needs to be said, except 'don't lose sight of Jesus'.

Epiphany

One of the great advantages of an Epiphany service is that it takes place at the beginning of the Spring term. It also provides a vital link between the birth of Jesus and the rest of his earthly ministry and passion. The taking down of decorations and Christmas trees can give a sense of putting the Christian faith away for next year (which is what many people do). Emphasis should be placed instead on the fact that Jesus' birth was only the start of God's plan for the salvation of mankind. Some traditions (notably the Eastern ones) use the Epiphany to celebrate Jesus' baptism, which highlights the neglected value of this Christian festival. It also fits well with the start of a new term and new year.

HYMNS

Traditional
Brightest and Best
As with gladness
The race that long in darkness
Christ is the world's light
Earth has many a noble city
Glorious things of thee are spoken
O worship the Lord
Awake, awake fling off the night
We three kings
Thou didst leave thy throne

Modern
You are the King of Glory
God of glory, we exalt your name
Worthy, O worthy
The light of Christ
From the sun's rising
All earth was dark
Darkness like a shroud
King of Kings and Lord of Lords
His name is Wonderful
Light has dawned

READINGS

Isaiah 41:8-20/42:1-9/49:1-6,7-13/60:1-6/Ephesians 3:1-6/1 John 1:1-4/Revelation 21:22-22:5/Matthew 2:1-12/Luke 2:41-52/John 1:29-34.

CONFESSION

Lord Jesus, you were worshipped by wise men who travelled far to seek you, and brought costly gifts at your birth. We too have seen your glory, but confess that it has not moved us to worship and sacrifice. We are sorry that we have failed to offer you our gifts or acknowledge you fully as our king. We ask you to forgive us, and help us to worship you in spirit and in truth, that your glory may shine through us and be revealed to the world around, through the love of our Saviour Jesus Christ. Amen.

Almighty God, who shows mercy to all who turn to him, forgive you for all your sins and failings and give you his peace and confidence through Christ our Lord. Amen.

PRAYER

As we kneel before the Son of God with the wise men, we pray to our heavenly Father, saying,
Lord, in your mercy,
Hear our prayer.

We pray for ourselves and all Christian people, that as we come before our Saviour we may worship him in spirit and in truth. Help us to acknowledge him as Lord and Saviour.
Lord, in your mercy,
Hear our prayer.

We pray for our world, and all who suffer as a result of man's inhumanity

to man. You left Heaven's glory for our sake to live in poverty. Help us to demonstrate your compassion and love for all who are weak and powerless.
Lord, in your mercy,
Hear our prayer.

We pray for our families, friends and our school community here. You shared the life of an earthly family and understand the joys and sadnesses of everyday relationships. Help us to show your love to those who are close to us, and to treat our families with respect.
Lord, in your mercy,
Hear our prayer.

We pray for ourselves, that we may offer back to you the gifts you've bestowed on us. Help us to use them to your glory, so that the whole world may come to see the beauty of your eternal Kingdom.
Lord, in your mercy,
Hear our prayer and accept our offering of ourselves for the sake of your Son, our Saviour Jesus Christ. Amen.

SERMON IDEA
Make up a gift-wrapped present from a largish cardboard box. Inside it place pieces of paper or card, wrapped up, on which are written some of God's gifts to us. You could include some of Paul's list in 1 Corinthians 12 or Romans 13, to highlight our responsibilities to use God's gifts in his church. However, you could take a different tack and talk about our personal abilities (music, art, organising, games, etc) and how we can use them to God's glory and for the benefit of all. Then there are gifts of creation – food, homes, life itself. We would have none of these things but for God's generosity (a surprising thought to many in our self-reliant, 'me first' society). As a parting shot, if time and space permit, give out a piece of paper to everyone and get them to write on it what they are willing to offer to God (however small they may think it is) and bring it up to the altar or a suitable equivalent as an act of commitment. By parallelling this with the gifts of the wise men you can underscore the meaning of the story. Epiphany is a good time to stress that just as Jesus went on to the Cross, so we too must demonstrate our dedication to his Kingdom.

LENT, HOLY WEEK & EASTER

With all the hype that surrounds us at Christmas, it's easy to forget that for the early Christians Easter was far and away the most important Christian festival. Many people would regard Easter as the more 'religious' festival, in that it's not been engulfed by quite such a large tidal wave of materialism as Christmas. There are still plenty of false impressions at large, however. One child recently informed me that Lent was a time 'when we all have to be miserable' – further research indicated that this was due to the whole family giving up chocolate and sweets for six weeks. It appeared that this self-denial had little Christian motivation. 'We always do it for Lent' was the reason given, which no doubt accounts for the boy viewing it as the most miserable time of the year. Easter eggs, Easter bunnies and extraordinary headgear can also threaten to cloud, if not totally obscure, the message of the greatest Christian festival.

The emphasis in Lent can well be placed on growing (which parallels what's happening in nature). Fasting certainly has spiritual value when undertaken for the right reasons, but 'giving up' something will mean little to most children other than dieting for better health. Maundy Thursday (which occasionally falls in term-time) is a splendid opportunity to teach children about Holy Communion, while Palm Sunday provides an ideal slot for a procession or celebration. Children love a story, and the events of Jesus' trial and crucifixion come alive when acted out. The resurrection is full of symbolism about new life, but Jesus' victory over sin and death can also bring home to people that this isn't just a happy ending to an otherwise sad story – it makes a difference to our lives *here and now*. To round off this season why not take advantage of Ascension Day? It usually falls in term-time, and as well as underlining the kingship of Christ, leads up to Pentecost.

Many schools like to pick up on the important days and seasons of the Church's year. The period from Ash Wednesday to Ascension Day is rich with such symbolism and scope for bringing the Christian message to those who aren't familiar with it. At its centre lies the heart of our faith. As we focus on Jesus' death and resurrection, people are drawn to him and his incredible love.

Ash Wednesday

The burning of ashes on Ash Wednesday is a powerful symbol, even for smaller children. The burned palm crosses can be a picture of the destruction of our old life with all that's wrong in it and spoils it. They can also remind us that all our past 'clutter' of wrong actions and words has been dealt with by the fire of God's purity and love. Whether or not you choose to impose the ashes on people's foreheads, emphasise that this day is about repentance and forgiveness. Extend this to demonstrate how God through his Son gives us a completely new start, which is why in Lent we put a special effort into growing in our spiritual lives.

HYMNS
Traditional

Amazing Grace
Father in Heaven whose love
Jesus, Lover of my soul
Just as I am
My faith looks up to thee
There's a wideness in God's mercy
All to Jesus I surrender
O love that will not let me go
With joy we meditate the grace
O Jesus, I have promised

Modern

Can it be true?
Cleanse me from my sin
O Lord the clouds are gathering
River, wash over me
Lord of the Cross of shame
Restore O Lord
Who can sound the depths of sorrow
Spirit of the living God
Come see the beauty of the Lord
Reign in me

READINGS
Isaiah 58:1-8, 1:11- 20/Joel 2:12-17
Amos 5:6-15/Ezekiel 18:21-22,30b-end/
1 Corinthians 9:24-end/2 Corinthians
5:20-6:2/James 4:1-10/Matthew 6:1-6,
16-18 (21)/Luke 18:9-14.

CONFESSION

We come before Jesus our Saviour, acknowledging our wrongdoing and need of his forgiveness, saying,
Create in us clean hearts, O Lord,
And renew a right spirit in us.

Father, we have done what is evil in your sight and offended you by our words, our deeds and the thoughts that lie behind them. Our lives have been spoiled by our rebelliousness and pride. Only you can save and restore us.
Create in us clean hearts, O Lord,
And renew a right spirit in us.

Father, as your people we have not obeyed your commands. We have not witnessed as we should to your saving love, nor proclaimed your glory to the world. Only you can forgive and strengthen us.
Create in us clean hearts, O Lord,
And renew a right spirit in us.

Father, as members of your kingdom we have not stood up for your standards of peace and justice in our world. We have closed our eyes to the suffering and poverty around us. Only you can pardon and deliver us.
Create in us clean hearts, O Lord,
And renew a right spirit within us.

Father, as members of your family we have not considered the wellbeing of those around us, or showed your compassion to them. Only you can cleanse and heal us.

Create in us clean hearts, O Lord,
And renew a right spirit within us.
Wash away our iniquities
and open our mouths
to declare the praise
of him who died for us,
Jesus Christ our Lord. Amen.

PRAYER

We come before our Saviour trusting in his mercy, saying,
Lord, in your mercy,
Hear our prayer.

We bring to the mercy of Christ our church, and God's people throughout this world . . . Help us to bear witness to your saving love.
Lord, in your mercy,
Hear our prayer.

We bring to the mercy of Christ our needy world, and those who govern it . . . Help us to bear witness to your caring justice.
Lord, in your mercy,
Hear our prayer.

We bring to the mercy of Christ our school and friends . . . Help us to bear witness to your forgiving grace.
Lord, in your mercy,
Hear our prayer.

We bring to the mercy of Christ anyone known to us who's suffering from illness, loneliness or sadness . . . Help us to bear witness to your healing power.
Lord, in your mercy,
Hear our prayer.

We bring to the mercy of Christ our own lives . . . Help us to bear witness to your coming Kingdom.
Lord, in your mercy,
Hear our prayer, and graciously
answer us when we call upon you, for
the love of your Son, Jesus our
Saviour. Amen.

SERMON IDEA

Find a fairly young plant and if possible transfer it to a large pot (a crocus or daffodil that hasn't flowered is ideal). Take some medium-sized garden stones and with poster paint write the name of a sin or wrong attitude, such as hatred, anger, dishonesty, stealing, cheating, etc. It's best to relate these to what the children would be familiar with (e.g. sexual sins will register with teenagers, but not with under-11's). Pile the painted stones carefully around the plant until it's obscured. Then get a child to remove one stone at a time and read out the word. Explain how the stones must be removed if the plant is to grow, and parallel this with how sins need to be dealt with if we are to grow properly as human beings.

Palm Sunday

Unless you're responsible for a boarding school, Palm Sunday will probably be celebrated on a weekday. A procession from school to the local church is a very effective idea where this is possible (for larger private schools a procession around the grounds to the chapel would be an alternative). All the participants should be encouraged to sing well-known hymns loudly and enthusiastically, and you may like to distribute palm crosses to wave before setting out. If there's a choir or music group, make sure they're placed in the middle of the procession, so that both ends can hear simultaneously. As I write this I'm preparing to take part in one with a real donkey – but you may feel this is taking realism too far! When the procession is over, the talk can be effectively based on the aftermath, as the crowd turns on Jesus and he is condemned to death. The symbolism of the donkey from Zechariah should be explained, especially if using a live animal. Children will be so fascinated by it that they may not otherwise register its significance.

HYMNS

Traditional
All glory, laud and honour
Ride on, ride on in majesty
Children of Jerusalem
The Lord is King
At the name of Jesus
My song is love unknown
The royal banners forward go
Praise to the holiest
We sing the praise of him who died

Modern
Give me oil in my lamp
Hosanna, hosanna!
Lift up your heads to the coming king

You are the King of glory
Make way, make way
Majesty
Jesus, name above all names
We cry Hosanna Lord!
Name of all majesty

READINGS

Psalm 118:15-21/Isaiah 62:10-12/Zechariah 9:9-12/Philippians 2:5-11/Hebrews 2:5-9/Matthew 21:1-11/Mark ll:l-l0/Luke 19:28-40/ (Psalm 24 also).

CONFESSION

On Palm Sunday,
the crowds worshipped Jesus;
on Good Friday they shouted for him to die. Let us who also worship him, confess that we sometimes reject him, and ask his forgiveness:

Lord Jesus Christ, you come to us in peace, but we shut the door of our mind against you.

In your mercy
Forgive and help us.

You come to us in humility, but we prefer our own proud ways.

In your mercy
Forgive us and help us.

You come to us in judgement, but we cling to our familiar sins.

In your mercy
Forgive us and help us.

You come to us in majesty, but we will not have you to reign over us.

In your mercy
Forgive us and help us.

Lord, forgive our empty praise, fill our loveless hearts;

come to us and make our lives your home for ever. Amen.

From *Church Family Worship*

PRAYER

We come to Jesus our King and ask his blessing on us, saying,

King Jesus, we welcome you;
Come and reign among us.

We ask you to bless our world, and to bring your peace to the places where violence rules . . .

King Jesus, we welcome you;
Come and reign among us.

We ask you to bless our school, and to bring your joy as we seek to obey you . . .

King Jesus, we welcome you;
Come and reign among us.

We ask you to bless your church, and all who bring relief and peace in your name . . .

King Jesus, we welcome you;
Come and reign among us.

We ask you to bless our families and homes, and to bring your love as we share our lives . . .

King Jesus, we welcome you;
Come and reign among us.

We ask you to bless those who are suffering and in pain, whether in body or mind, and to bring your healing and comfort . . .

King Jesus, we welcome you;
Come and reign among us. Bring your blessing to our hearts and lives and fill them always with your praises, through Jesus Christ our Lord, to whom we cry 'Hosanna in the Highest'. Amen.

SERMON IDEA

Start by talking about the unexpected happening. We all have certain expectations based on what usually happens (in our experience!). Proceed to demonstrate how this can be overturned and confused with visual aids. It's possible to buy proprietary conjuring tricks to achieve this, such as a 'solid' plastic screen through which you can push a pencil. The only disadvantage is that such gags need to be thoroughly practised beforehand, and may become the focal point of the talk unless great care is taken. An effective alternative is to take an empty milk bottle and fill it with white emulsion paint. When emptied it should look 'full'. Preserve a metallised top carefully, fill the empty bottle with water, and cap it. From a distance, emptying it can cause a great stir.

Another idea is to put a valuable object into some very tatty wrapping so that its value is only revealed when the packaging is discarded. Use this to show how Jesus wasn't the kind of King anyone was expecting. He didn't try to take over the government, he didn't live in a palace or wear nice clothes and he had no money or influence. Instead of recognising that he really was a king, they crucified him because he didn't do what they wanted. Just as the scruffy wrapping could have been discarded with the valuable object inside, so Jesus was rejected by his contemporaries. Point out how we can reject Jesus for the wrong reasons. He doesn't exist to do just what we want. He's the King of Kings; we receive him as that and obey him gladly.

Holy Week (Jesus' Trial)

1 Peter 2:21-25/Matthew 26:57-68/
27:11-31/Luke 22:66-23:25
John 18:28-19:1.

Holy Week doesn't always fall in term-time, but when it does it gives a great opportunity to look at Jesus' trial. Alternatively, when term finishes earlier, it can be a good subject for the end of term service. Because it's so dramatic, there's good scope for this narrative being used as drama and the 'Lent, Holy Week and Easter' book of services dramatises the passion narratives of all four gospels. For older children this can almost replace a sermon. However, you may want to emphasise how unfair Jesus' trial was and how cruel his punishment, in which case it's essential to explain why Jesus went through with it, knowing what would happen, in obedience to his Father.

Hymns

Traditional

It is a thing most wonderful
My song is love unknown
My God! I love thee
Man of Sorrows!
Ah, holy Jesus
We sing the praise of him who died
Glory be to Jesus
When I survey the wondrous Cross

Modern

He stood before the court
Lord of the Cross of shame
Empty he came
You laid aside your majesty
The price is paid
Meekness and majesty
He was pierced for our transgressions
Thank you for the Cross

Readings

Psalm 27:7-end/Isaiah 50:4-9/52:13-53:end/Acts 8:26 -40/Philippians 2:5-11

Confession

Loving Father, your Son was given the most unfair trial and cruel punishment, although he had done no wrong. We confess that we, too, have not listened to his voice or acknowledged his Lordship. Forgive us, we pray, for rejecting his claims on our lives, and give us your strength to stand by him and live as those who accept him as their King. In his name we ask this. Amen.

May God in his loving mercy forgive you for all your sins, restore you to himself, and strengthen you to live for him through Jesus Christ our Lord. Amen.

Prayer

We bring our prayers to Jesus, who was rejected and despised, saying,
Lord of love,
Hear our cry.

We pray for all your people around the world, especially in . . . May they show your compassion to all who feel unwanted and unloved.
Lord of love,
Hear our cry.

We pray for all in our society who have been forgotten or ignored . . . May we ever be mindful that your salvation is for everyone.
Lord of love,
Hear our cry.

We pray for all who suffer from injustice and oppression, especially . . .

May they know that you have shared their pain, and receive your peace.
Lord of love,
Hear our cry.

We pray for all who are ill in body or mind, especially . . . May they know your loving arms surrounding them.
Lord of love,
Hear our cry.

We pray for all who are anxious, lonely or in despair, especially . . . May they find in you their perfect friend.
Lord of love,
Hear our cry, and bring us all the joy of your salvation, through the love of Jesus Christ our Lord. Amen.

SERMON IDEA
There are many ways to get children to think (and usually say), 'That's not fair'. If there's a piano available ask for someone who can play it, and when they're sitting down give them a piece of music by Chopin or Liszt which could only be played by a virtuoso. Demand that they play it and if they can't, make critical comments and unkind jibes. It won't be long before everyone else is against you. Point out that you don't really mean it, but that we often make unfair judgements because we have the wrong expectations. (If no piano is nearby, borrow a flute or violin – the effect is the same.)

The people of Jesus' time were expecting a Messiah who would deliver them from the Romans and bring them material prosperity and political freedom. Jesus came to bring us the Kingdom of God, however. To do so he had to obey his Father's will, even to the extent of dying a criminal's death, so that we could be forgiven and set free from the tyranny of sin and death. If we expect Jesus to make us feel happy and comfortable, with no more problems, we'll be disappointed, and judge him unfairly. It's as we allow him to be in our lives all the time that we find he brings us God's peace and strength to face and overcome the problems of life.

Maundy Thursday

If Maundy Thursday falls during term-time, it will be the final day before the Easter break. Teaching about Holy Communion needs to be handled sensitively, most of all with younger children, but it can be introduced at any time towards the end of Lent. The extent to which you use the symbolism will depend on your tradition, but great care is required not to dwell on the qualifications for receiving bread and wine, especially in schools where there are children of many traditions and none.

In some circumstances it might be possible for everyone to share in the bread and wine, but this would cause many problems in the Anglican and Roman Catholic traditions. The alternatives are to give the elements only to adults, only to those who are already confirmed, or to handle it in some other way. Children need to ask 'Why?', and will do so mentally if not verbally. Why bread and wine? Why dress up for it? Why are some excluded? Why remember something that happened two thousand years ago? These are questions that must be addressed in some way if they aren't to become a barrier to understanding and acceptance.

HYMNS

Traditional

Bread of Heaven, on thee we feed
Jesus, thou joy of loving hearts
Author of life divine
My God and is thy table spread
And now, O Father, mindful of the love
Alleluia, sing to Jesus
O Thou, who at thy eucharist
We hail thy presence glorious
Here, O my Lord, I see thee face to face
We come as guests invited

Modern

A new commandment
Broken for me
Make me a channel of your peace
I am the bread of life
We break this bread
Let us break bread together
There is a redeemer
He was pierced for our transgressions
He gave his life
You are the vine

READINGS

Exodus 12:1-14/Psalm 105:37-45/
Isaiah 48:17-21/1 Corinthians 11:23-29/
Hebrews 10:19-25/1 John 4:7-14/
Matthew 26:17-30/Mark 14:12-26/
Luke 22:7- 23 (or 30)/John 13:1-15.

CONFESSION

Almighty God, your Son Jesus Christ came to be the servant of all and to give his life as a ransom for many. We have acted out of self-interest and not followed his way of service and sacrifice. Cleanse us from our selfish attitudes and deliver us from narrow prejudice, that we may follow the example of our Saviour and live to the glory of your name. Amen.

Almighty God, who has mercy on all who truly turn to him, grant unto you pardon for all your sins, time to repent and turn to him, and the strength to walk in his way of perfect freedom. Amen.

PRAYER

We bring to God our sacrifice of thanksgiving, saying,
Lord, in your glory,
Accept our praise.

We thank you for your gift of creation, which mirrors your nature. In gratitude

May the Father of all mercies
cleanse you from your sins,
and restore you to his service
for the praise and glory of his name
through Jesus Christ our Lord. **Amen.**

Adapted from *Church Family Worship*

The book of services for Lent, Holy Week and Easter includes four
anthems for Good Friday under the heading 'Proclamation of the Cross'.
The second of these, although long, is very suitable, especially if as
suggested, a simple wooden cross is displayed while the congregation
joins in the responses. Best used with older children or teenagers, it's a
powerful alternative to the usual style of confession.

PRAYER

We come before our Saviour as he lays
down his life for us on the Cross, saying,

Lord, hear our prayer,
And let our cry come to you.

We thank you that on the Cross you
were willing to forgive those who hated
and condemned you to death. Please
help all who ill-treat others for personal
gain to recognise that only by accepting
your love will they find themselves.

Lord, hear our prayer,
And let our cry come to you.

We thank you that you showed compassion even from the cross. Please give
strength and comfort to all who share
your love with the suffering and lonely.

Lord, hear our prayer,
And let our cry come to you.

We thank you that the penitent thief
received your forgiveness as he
acknowledged your Kingship. Please
bring your peace to all who feel
rejected, and unworthy of your love.

Lord, hear our prayer,
And let our cry come to you.

We thank you that you were willing to
be obedient, even to death on the
Cross. Please help us to follow your
example of selfless love and service.

Lord, hear our prayer.

And let our cry come to you.

We thank you that by your death, you
won for us eternal life. Please help us
to live in the power of your
resurrection, that your glory may be
seen throughout the world.

Lord, hear our prayer,
**And let our cry come to you. As you
have loved us, so may we receive your
grace to love one another for the sake
of him who died for us, Jesus Christ
our Lord. Amen.**

SERMON IDEA

This idea comes from *For All The Family*.
Either on an OHP acetate sheet or on a
large piece of card draw a cross, with
the lengths of both lines equal. Having
asked how this symbol is used, pick on
three answers. It can be an indication in
a maths book that a question has been
answered wrongly. Produce on a large
sheet of card or paper a simple
arithmetical miscalculation marked
wrong. The Cross of Jesus is also an
indication that we have done wrong –
unkind words, selfish actions, cruel
thoughts; Jesus' Cross marks them all
wrong.

If the first cross is turned through 90
degrees it becomes a 'kiss'. Here show
the inside of a Valentine card which
says, 'I love you. XXXXXX'. Jesus' Cross
is a sign of love, too. His love for us is
so great that he would stop at nothing
to bring us back to him. He still says to
us 'I love you', and the Cross proves it.
The third use of a cross is illustrated by
a red triangle with a cross inside it,
indicating a road junction ahead where
we have to decide which way to go.
Jesus' Cross forces us into deciding
which way to go, too. Are we willing to
follow his way or our own way? We
can't avoid making that decision.

Easter
(Resurrection)

Very few schools are likely to have an Easter Sunday service, but the themes of the greatest day in the Christian year can be brought out in the following weeks. It's a day of joy and happiness, a glorious victory celebration! Care should be taken to avoid the impression that the resurrection was God's happy ending to a story that otherwise would have come to a tragic conclusion. The resurrection was as much part of God's plan as the rest of Jesus' life and ministry. By raising him to new and unending life God the Father vindicated all that his Son had done and achieved. Into a world full of gloom and despair the risen Jesus brings hope and light, and enables us to share his resurrection life. It has to be recognised that for some this will be an unhappy time, because of personal experiences or memories. Sensitivity to their feelings should not cloud the message that the marvellous light of the risen Christ penetrates even the darkest situation.

HYMNS

Traditional
Christ is risen, Hallelujah!
Christ the Lord is risen today
Jesus Christ is risen today
Jesus lives, thy terrors now
The head that once was crowned
Thine be the glory
Christ the Lord is risen again
The day of resurrection
This joyful Eastertime
Now the green blade riseth

Modern
Led like a lamb to the slaughter
All Heaven declares
For this purpose
Jesus is Lord

Come sing the praise of Jesus
Come and see the shining hope
The price is paid
At your feet we fall
He is Lord
Alleluia, alleluia, give thanks

READINGS

Job 19:21-27/Psalm 118:14-24/
Exodus 14:15-end/Isaiah 12/43:
16-21/Hosea 6:1-6/Romans 6:3-11/
1 Corinthians 15:12-20/Revelation 1:10-
18/Matthew 28:1-10/Mark 16:1-8
(or 10)/Luke 24:1-12 /John 20:1-10.

CONFESSION

Living Lord, raised from death and victorious over evil, we come to you with our weakness and failures. We confess that our lives are too often spoiled by fear and unbelief; that we have lived in our own strength instead of trusting the power of your risen life. Forgive us, we pray, and by your great mercy set our minds on the things which are above, that we may declare the glory of your resurrection and live in your marvellous light, through our Lord and Saviour, Jesus Christ. Amen.

PRAYER

Our Lord Jesus Christ, risen from death, we praise you for changed lives and new hopes at Easter.

You came to Mary in the garden, and turned her tears into joy.

For your love and your mercy,
We give you thanks, O Lord.

You came to the disciples in the upper room, and turned their fear into courage.

For your love and your mercy,
We give you thanks, O Lord.

You came to the disciples by the lake-side, and turned their failure into faith.
For your love and your mercy,
We give you thanks, O Lord.

You came to the disciples on the Emmaus road, and turned their despair into hope.
For your love and your mercy,
We give you thanks, O Lord.

You come to us in our unworthiness and shame, and turn our weakness into triumph.
For your love and your mercy,
We give you thanks, O Lord.

Lord Jesus, wherever there are tears, or fear, or failure, or despair, or weakness: come, reveal to us your love, your mercy, and your risen power; for the glory of your name.
Alleluia! Amen.

SERMON IDEA

Although we all celebrate Easter as a holiday, and may even enjoy it as an opportunity for a trip to church, many people aren't really open either to the truth that God raised his Son from death, or that this can transform their lives. By emphasising the need for openness, not just to the truth but ultimately to the risen Lord himself, Easter is underlined as the very heart of our faith. If you can obtain the services of an artist, pictures of the various characters and scenes can bring this to life.

Alternatively, you could persuade some of the children to mime the parts concerned (or even act them if you have time to produce a short script).

The first person to see Jesus after his resurrection was Mary, in the garden. Not surprisingly, she thought he must be the gardener – her eyes were blurred with tears, so she didn't recognise him. Her ears were open, however, and she heard him speak her name. We need to open our eyes and ears if we are to recognise him and hear him calling our name.

A bit later, along came Peter and John and discovered, much to their amazement, that the stone had been rolled away from the tomb. John stopped at the entrance, but Peter just tore straight in. The open tomb was an open door. Jesus' resurrection is an open door to new and eternal life for all who are willing to go through it. (If you have a conveniently placed door and a willing actor the symbolism can have a considerable impact.)

Then there's Thomas, who wasn't around when Jesus appeared to the others, and found it hard to believe them. He needed an open mind to accept the evidence of the rest of the disciples, but refused to believe until he saw Jesus for himself. As a final point bring in all the disciples, out on the lake and fed up after a long night's unsuccessful fishing. They had to open their hands to receive the great catch that Jesus gave them. We, too, need to open our hands spiritually to receive the blessings that God gives us by his Holy Spirit.

Easter
The Emmaus Road

If Easter Sunday is too far away from the beginning of term, the Emmaus Road is a useful vehicle for conveying the truth of the resurrection. Many folk will assent to a belief in the resurrection of Jesus, but like those two disciples find it hard to recognise him. The significance of the breaking of the bread can be drawn out in terms of receiving Communion; or the return of the two disciples in sheer excitement to spread the good news could be an encouragement to personal evangelism. There's a lot of personal experience in this account, but it's also important to see how the risen Jesus speaks to the two from the Scriptures. Many at a school service are likely to have little in the way of personal faith. They need to understand that this isn't all based on emotion but on fact.

HYMNS
Traditional
I know that my redeemer lives
At the Lamb's high feast
Love's redeeming work is done
Jesus, stand among us
I come with joy to meet my Lord
Bread of Heaven on Thee we feed
Through the night of doubt and sorrow
We have a gospel to proclaim
Crown him with many crowns
Lord, enthroned in heavenly splendour

Modern
O what a gift
I am the bread of life
All hail the Lamb!
Let us talents and tongues employ
Thank you Jesus
Meekness and majesty
Open our eyes Lord
I want to walk with Jesus Christ

He that is in us
Jesus stand among us at the meeting
   of our lives

READINGS
Numbers 21:4-9/Isaiah 40:9-11/Micah 7:14-20/1 Peter 1:3-12/1 Corinthians 15:20-28/Acts 17:16-31/Luke 24:13-35.

CONFESSION
Living Lord Jesus, you appeared to your followers on the way to Emmaus, yet they failed to recognise you. We acknowledge that we too have not always opened our eyes to see you, nor our ears to listen to you. Forgive our slowness and blindness, and give us the vision to recognise and welcome you with joy into our lives. This we ask in your name. Amen.

Almighty God, who raised from the dead our Lord Jesus, forgive you all your sins, and strengthen you to walk with him in joy and confidence, through the risen Christ. Amen.

PRAYER
In joy and confidence we pray to our risen Saviour, saying,
Risen Master,
In your mercy, hear us.

We ask that you will fill all your people with the power of your resurrection life. Especially we pray for Christians who are suffering because of persecution, isolation or poverty . . .
Risen Master,
In your mercy, hear us.

We ask that you will fill us with the truth of your resurrection life.
Especially we pray that your people will be bold to declare the good news of eternal life to our needy world . . .

Risen Master,
In your mercy, hear us.

We ask that you will fill us with the peace of your resurrection life. Especially we pray for those suffering through violence, exploitation or injustice, and for the leaders of the nations . . .
Risen Master,
In your mercy, hear us.

We ask that you will fill us with the comfort of your resurrection life. Especially we pray for those who are suffering from ill-health of body or mind, from anxiety or fear, from bereavement or loneliness . . .
Risen Master,
In your mercy, hear us.

We ask that you will fill us with the joy of your resurrection life. Especially we pray that with our lips and lives we will proclaim the praises of Jesus your Son, our Saviour . . .
Risen Master,
In your mercy, hear us and receive our prayers. Amen.

SERMON IDEA

With younger children the theme of recognising someone can be illustrated by using pictures of well-known personalities, suitably 'disguised' with a felt-tipped pen. Discuss the ways in which we do recognise someone – by their face, for example. If we have not seen a friend for a long while, or someone we know has had a drastic change of hairstyle, it may take us a few moments to work out who's greeted us.

After his resurrection Jesus had changed a great deal, and the disciples needed other ways of recognising him. We also identify a voice. Even on the telephone some people have an unmistakable way of speaking. The disciples on the road to Emmaus, perhaps, thought there was something familiar in what they were hearing, but they couldn't quite catch what was familiar about it. (This is well illustrated with a tape-recording of well-known voices, either from the radio or of staff members.)

They finally realised who Jesus was when they shared a meal with him and he gave thanks for it. In fact, they needn't have invited this stranger in at all – but if they hadn't, they would never have discovered who he was. We recognise people because of our relationship with them. It's not just looks and voices, but the sort of person we know they are. We may hear Jesus speaking to us and see evidence of him around us or in our lives but if we don't enter into a relationship with him we'll never realise who he is.

Ascension

Ascension Day marks the end of the ministry on earth of Jesus. His work on earth has been completed, and he has done all that his Father gave him to accomplish. The resurrection was the Father's vindication of His Son. The ascension is his glorification. Jesus returned to his Father in glory and now reigns for ever at his right hand. Ascension isn't the end, however, but the beginning, because Jesus had promised his disciples and all who follow him and own him as their king that they would receive the gift of the Holy Spirit, the living presence of the risen Lord with us for ever. He also promised that, just as he'd returned to Heaven, so one day he would come back in the same way, in glory. It's a day for looking forward, as well as back.

The theme of Jesus' kingship, reigning in glory and in our hearts, is a powerful one, though you could equally emphasise the promises of Jesus – in particular the promise of the Holy Spirit is a good preparation for Pentecost. Encourage plenty of praise and celebration. Some schools go outdoors for this service, to the top of a local hill. This is an excellent idea, but needs careful thought to ensure audibility and concentration.

HYMNS

Traditional

All hail the power of Jesus' name
Alleluia, sing to Jesus
Crown him with many crowns
Hail the day that sees him rise
King of glory, King of peace
Lord, enthroned in heavenly splendour
See, the conqueror mounts in triumph
Rejoice, the Lord is King!
Jesus shall reign where'er the sun
We have a gospel to proclaim

Modern

Ascended Christ
Christ triumphant
Jesus is King, and I will extol him
Worthy, O worthy are you, Lord
God of glory, we exalt your name
Jesus shall take the highest honour
From the sun's rising
We see the Lord
How lovely on the mountains
He is exalted

READINGS

2 Samuel 23:1-5 / Psalm 21:1-7 / Isaiah 52:7-10 / Acts 1:1-11 / Ephesians 2:4-10 / Hebrews 2:4-10 / Matthew 28:16-end / Mark 16:14-end / Luke 24:45-end.

CONFESSION

Lord Jesus, you gave your life for us on the Cross, yet we have not loved you with all our hearts. You were raised from the dead as victor over sin and death, yet we have not lived in the light of eternal life. You returned to Heaven in glory, yet we have not worshipped you as our King. Pardon and deliver us, we pray, and fill us with a new joy in worship and a new obedience to your will, for the sake of your glorious Kingdom. Amen.

Almighty God, the Father of our Lord Jesus Christ, grant unto you forgiveness of all your sins and strength in your weakness, that you may live in accordance with his will, to his praise and glory. Amen.

PRAYER

Let us pray to the King of Kings, the sovereign ruler and creator of all that is, saying,
Lord of glory,
Hear your people's prayer.

We bring before you all Christian people, members of your eternal Kingdom. In joy or sorrow, in peace or turmoil, in poverty or wealth, may we worship you as our Lord and serve you as our Master.

Lord of glory,
Hear your people's prayer.

We bring before you this world, and all who have authority over it. Reign in the hearts of those who govern and direct, that the justice and righteousness of your Kingdom may be seen on earth.

Lord of glory,
Hear your people's prayer.

We bring before you our school, and all who teach or learn there. In lessons or in leisure reign in our hearts and help us to make it a glimpse of your eternal kingdom.

Lord of glory,
Hear your people's prayer.

We bring before you our families and friends, and all who suffer pain, fear or loneliness. Be present with them and help them to recognise you as the sovereign Lord in control of all their circumstances.

Lord of glory,
Hear your people's prayer.

We bring before you our own lives. Make us obedient to your will, and fill our hearts with praise to our eternal King.

Lord of glory,
Hear your people's prayer, and reign among us as King of Kings, for your glory's sake. Amen.

SERMON IDEA

Some people just have to have the last word! That's because last words are most easily remembered. Before the service give out a few 'famous last words', written on a piece of card, to members of the congregation.

Start off by talking about last words, and then ask those with the quotations to read them out, one at a time. Some good suggestions are: the end of King Lear, the end of Becket's Christmas sermon in *Murder in the Cathedral,* or the last words of Poirot in an Agatha Christie novel. Stress how it's the final words that we hold in our minds. That's why parents tell their children to be good when they set out without them! Jesus wanted his friends to remember what he had said, so he left his promises to the very end of his time on earth. He promised that by his Holy Spirit he'd be with them for ever, and that one day he'd return in glory to this world. He also told them that until he returned they were to tell others the good news, and make them his disciples. The Holy Spirit is the promise of his presence with us as we share that good news with those around us.

PENTECOST

Unlike Christmas and Easter, Pentecost remains commercially insignificant. There's no run-up to it to compare with Advent or Lent, apart from being an excuse for a half-term holiday (in name at least), it's a purely church-based festival. Its impact is also quite different from Christmas and Easter. There's something very moving about the infancy narratives, and real drama in the Passion and Resurrection accounts. By contrast the day of Pentecost consists of little in the way of a story – its importance lies in the birth of the Christian church as a result. The Holy Spirit isn't an easy concept to grasp, either. God our heavenly Father is at least comprehensible, while Jesus came so that we could relate to him, and through him to God. But the Holy Spirit can seem rather vague and obscure, more for those given to 'ecstatic trances and wild imaginings'.

The Church has long failed to provide a balanced teaching about the Holy Spirit as the third person of the Godhead. Consequently there are many misunderstandings about who he is and why God gives him to us. The symbolism of fire and wind is strong, but the Biblical teaching about the gifts and the fruits of the Holy Spirit should also be emphasised. Many will try to interpret them as a moral code, but the emphasis should be on the Spirit producing these patterns of behaviour as he lives within us. Trinity is also included in this section. It's a topic most of us dread preaching on to adults, let alone explaining to children. However, it's a vital part of Christian teaching for a balanced understanding of God.

The Day of Pentecost

If you ask many children (and adults, for that matter) about the significance of the Day of Pentecost, the most likely answer would be the 'birthday of the Church'. It is certainly true, to the extent that the first significant grouping of believers came together on that day, and from then on the Christian Church grew rapidly and spread throughout the Middle East before moving on to Europe, Africa and Asia. As a result, believers today meet for worship and fellowship right across the world – and if Christianity seems pretty marginal to our society, it's increasing mightily in parts of Africa, South America and Asia (notably South Korea).

Yet the initial impact was on twelve frightened, uneducated men, none of whom would have been regarded even as 'dark horses' to become founders of the largest single network of religious adherents in the world. The questions to ask are 'what happened to make them what they became?' and 'what difference did this extraordinary experience make to their lives?' It's that difference which transforms our lives, too. Outside a church context, the birthday celebrations theme may not fit (could be great in a Church school, though – why not make a special cake or have a party?). The effects of the Holy Spirit's coming have significance for us now. Those who recognise it are able to influence society in the ways of God's Kingdom.

HYMNS
Traditional
Breathe on me, Breath of God
Come down, O love divine
Come, Holy Ghost, our souls inspire
O breath of life
Love divine, all loves excelling
Gracious Spirit, Holy Ghost
O thou who camest from above
O Holy Spirit, breathe on me
Our blest Redeemer
Holy Spirit, come confirm us

Modern
All over the world
Spirit of God, unseen as the wind
Spirit of the living God
Spirit of God, show me Jesus
Fear not, rejoice and be glad
He that is in us
Wind, wind, blow on me
There's a spirit in the air
The Spirit lives to set us free
Holy Spirit, we welcome you.

READINGS
Genesis 11:1-9/Ezekiel 37:1-14/Joel 2:21-end/Acts 2:1-ll/Romans 8:18-27/ 1 Corinthians 12:1-11/John 14:15-26/ 16: 5-16/20:19 -23.

CONFESSION
Spirit of Jesus, you came upon the disciples in wind and flame, filling them with your power and authority. Forgive us, we ask you, that our lives show little evidence of your power within, and our witness little sign of your authority. Fill us anew with the power of your Spirit that our tongues may be loosened to declare your gospel, and our lives released to reveal its power, through Jesus Christ our Lord. Amen.

Almighty God, whose Spirit comes upon all who will receive him, grant unto you forgiveness for your sins, peace in your hearts, and power to live for him day by day, through Christ our Lord. Amen.

PRAYER

We pray for God to fill us with his
Spirit, saying,

Lord, come to bless us,
And fill us with your Spirit.

Generous God, we thank you for the
power of your Holy Spirit. We ask that
we may be strengthened to serve you
better.

Lord, come to bless us,
And fill us with your Spirit.

We thank you for the wisdom of your
Holy Spirit. We ask you to help us
understand better your will for us.

Lord, come to bless us,
And fill us with your Spirit.

We thank you for the peace of your
Holy Spirit. We ask you to keep us
confident of your love and strength
wherever you call us to serve you.

Lord, come to bless us,
And fill us with your Spirit.

We thank you for the gifts of your Holy
Spirit. We ask you to equip us for the
work which you have given us.

Lord, come to bless us,
And fill us with your Spirit.

We thank you for the fruit of your Holy
Spirit. We ask you to help us to live
lives which are more pleasing to you
and show other people the love of
Jesus.

Lord, come to bless us,
And fill us with your Spirit.

Generous God, you sent your Holy
Spirit upon Christ at the river Jordan,
and upon the disciples at the feast of
Pentecost.

In your mercy, fill us with your Spirit.

**Hear our prayer, and make us one in
heart and mind to serve you in Christ
our Lord. Amen.**

From *Patterns for Worship*

SERMON IDEA

Wind and flames both symbolise
power. Start by explaining that power
can be frightening when out of control,
but useful when harnessed and
properly channelled. You could show a
picture of a powerful car, pointing out
that it needs to be driven properly to be
safe. An older age-group could benefit
from a discussion of the Chernobyl
accident, and the safe generation of
power.

An excellent visual aid is a length
of flex with no plug or appliance
attached, and the bare wires visible.
Point out that the wire is useless unless
the flex is connected to the power
source, and that it's both useless and
dangerous unless attached to a useful
appliance. Here you could produce an
iron, an electric kettle or a radio, which
can be demonstrated to the congregation. Explain that the Holy Spirit is
the power of God in our lives. We're
just channels to take him to a particular
purpose. It's also important to stress
that the Holy Spirit is a person, part of
the Godhead, and not just an abstract
force (which could easily be confused
with much New Age teaching).

Pentecost – The Gifts of the Spirit

After a long period when the Church ignored him for the most part, the Holy Spirit has made a comeback in the latter half of the twentieth century. Although this was initially within the Pentecostal tradition, almost all the mainstream churches have had to acknowledge the influence of the charismatic renewal. Many local churches of all traditions have experienced the Holy Spirit working among them, and coming in power to renew and revitalise their spiritual life, faith and witness. Part of the emphasis for these fellowships has been the 'every member ministry', in which each regular worshipper is encouraged and enabled to use their spiritual gifts for the benefit of the whole congregation and community. There are two important areas to distinguish:

1 *The sorts of gifts mentioned by Paul in some of his letters – pastoral, evangelistic, apostolic, prophetic and so on. While these may be aided by natural ability (e.g., at speaking in public), they are primarily spiritual both in nature and direction. David Watson, one of the greatest evangelists of this century, never regarded himself as a 'natural' for this. He prayed for the gift and received it, seeing it as spiritual in origin and purpose.*

2 *The natural talent which, when dedicated to God's service, can equally be used by the Holy Spirit to build up the church. Musical and artistic gifts, as well as the practical ones, come into this category.*

Bear in mind that every believer has some kind of spiritual gift; none should regard their contribution as superior (or more likely inferior) to someone else's.

HYMNS

Traditional
Take my life and let it be
Christ is our cornerstone
Let saints on earth in concert sing
Thy hand, O God, has guided
Ye that know the Lord is gracious
Holy Spirit, truth divine
Filled with the Spirit's power
Come, thou Holy Spirit, come
Eternal ruler of the ceaseless round
Gracious Spirit, Holy Ghost

Modern
Lord, make me an instrument
For I'm building
In our lives, Lord, be glorified
Let there be love shared among us
Rejoice, rejoice, Christ is in you
Let us talents and tongues employ
Falling, falling
God's Spirit is in my heart
Bind us together
The King is among us

READINGS

Exodus 31:1-11/2 Chronicles 34:8-13/Daniel 2:24-30/Romans 12: 1-8/1 Corinthians 12:4-11/27-31/1 Peter 4:7-ll/Matthew 10:1-10/25:14-30.

CONFESSION

Heavenly Father, you promised the gift of your Holy Spirit to all who believe and trust in your Son, Jesus Christ. We confess that we have not believed in him with all our hearts, nor trusted him fully. We have quenched your Spirit's work in our lives. Pardon our self-reliance and faithlessness, and so fill us with your power that the gifts of the Spirit alone may make us bold in witness and zealous in the service of Jesus Christ our Lord. Amen.

Almighty God, who shows mercy to all who turn to him in repentance and faith, forgive you for all your self-will and release the power of his Holy Spirit in your lives to the glory of his Son, Jesus Christ, our Lord. Amen.

PRAYER

Let us ask God for the gifts of his Spirit to be seen in our lives as we say,
Spirit of Jesus,
Fill our hearts.

We pray that we and all God's people may be bold to declare the truth of the Gospel and not be ashamed of it. Especially we ask . . .
Spirit of truth,
Fill our hearts.

We pray that as citizens of your Kingdom we may pursue the paths of peace and justice. Especially we ask . . .
Spirit of peace,
Fill our hearts.

We pray that in all our relationships, at home or at school, we may show the love and care of Jesus to those we meet. Especially we ask . . .
Spirit of love,
Fill our hearts.

We pray that anyone we know, suffering from illness, loneliness or anxiety at the moment will receive the comfort of the Holy Spirit. Especially we ask . . .
Spirit of healing,
Fill our hearts.

We pray for ourselves that our witness and service may be characterised not by a sense of duty but by the joy of the Lord. Especially we ask . . .
Spirit of joy,
Fill our hearts and transform our lives into the likeness of your Son, our Saviour Jesus Christ. Amen.

SERMON IDEA

The gifts of the Spirit are mentioned primarily in the context of teaching about the Body of Christ. If you can borrow a model skeleton from somewhere, it is very simple to demonstrate the importance of coordination. Every part needs to move in conjunction with the rest of the body, or it won't get anywhere. An alternative is to use a volunteer body, who won't mind being pulled and pushed a bit. Simple actions like walking, picking something up, eating a sweet, or threading a needle can vividly portray the way in which every part of our body must act in concert.

Explain that the Holy Spirit gives us all different gifts so that, like different parts of a body, we all play our part in its overall life and purpose. If one part tries to go it alone, the rest suffer. The gifts could be categorised as gifts of thinking, speaking and doing. If everyone was good at thinking, not much would be said or done. If there were only gifts of speaking much noise would emerge, but with no thought behind it or useful actions. If everyone was busy doing, nobody would think about what should be done or explain how to do it. No-one is more important or useful than anyone else. God has equipped each of us for whatever task he's called us to and it's up to us to use those gifts to serve him as he calls.

Pentecost – The Fruits of the Spirit

There may be disagreements over the gifts of the Holy Spirit, but no-one would argue about the fruits. The only danger is that they become nothing more than a moral code, a nice way to behave. It's true enough that the world would be a much happier place if we all displayed love, joy and peace without interruption, but we find that hard in our own families and homes, let alone anywhere else. The fruits of the Spirit are the result and evidence of faith in Christ, just as apples grow on apple trees because it's in the nature of an apple tree to produce apples, as opposed to pears or oranges. If Christ lives in us by his Spirit our lives will inevitably bear witness to this. The fruits of the Spirit are seen supremely in the life of Jesus, reflecting the character of his Father. The visual nature of this topic lends itself well to a children's talk, but beware of pitching it too low – moralising will lead to a misunderstanding of the Bible's teaching.

HYMNS

Traditional

Awake, awake, fling off the night
Love divine, all loves excelling
Christ, from whom all blessings flow
Lead us, heavenly Father, lead us
Born by the Holy Spirit's breath
Peace, perfect peace
In heavenly love abiding
Gracious Spirit, Holy Ghost
Teach me, my God and King

Modern

Make me a channel of your peace
Let there be love shared among us
Let there be peace on earth
A new commandment I give unto you

Seek ye the Lord, all you people
Send me out from here, Lord
My peace I give unto you
Peace to you
Give me joy in my heart

READINGS

Isaiah 5:1-7/32:14-17/Psalm 1/
Galatians 5:22-26/Ephesians 5:8-16/
Colossians 3:12-15/Matthew 7:16-23/
John 15:1-7.

CONFESSION

Heavenly Father, we are sorry that our lives do not always display the fruits of your Holy Spirit. Where love should reign, there is conflict; where joy should dominate there is despair; where peace should rule there is tension. Have mercy and pardon us for all wrong attitudes. Fill us with your Spirit, that our lives may reflect the character of Jesus and bear fruit which comes from repentance, for the sake of your Son, Jesus Christ our Saviour. Amen.

Almighty God, forgive you for all your sins and grant unto you a spirit of repentance, peace and joy as you walk with him. Amen.

PRAYER

As the Holy Spirit guides us, we come before our heavenly Father, saying,
Lord, make us holy,
And may our lives bear fruit for you.

The fruit of the Spirit is joy. May we delight in what is good and right, not complaining when things go wrong but rejoicing in your goodness, and trusting you to lead us in your way.
Lord, make us holy,
And may our lives bear fruit for you.

The fruit of the Spirit is peace. May we be peacemakers, not creating conflict or tension but demonstrating the reconciling love of Jesus in our lives.

Lord, make us holy,
And may our lives bear fruit for you.

The fruit of the Spirit is patience. May we face difficulty and hardship in your strength, not giving up or wavering in our faith, but allowing your will to be done in us.

Lord, make us holy,
And may our lives bear fruit for you.

The fruit of the Spirit is kindness. May we be those who recognise need and care for the needy, not putting our own interests first, but showing the compassion and love of Jesus.

Lord, make us holy,
And may our lives bear fruit for you.

The fruit of the Spirit is love. May we be filled with your love, not allowing self to rule our lives, but submitting to you as Lord, and witnessing to you as our Saviour and Friend.

Lord, make us holy,
And may our lives bear fruit for you, to the glory of your name. Amen.

SERMON IDEA
With younger age-groups this theme is tailor-made for strong visual aids. Either draw, or get someone gifted at art to draw for you, nine pieces of fruit on large pieces of card. They could be selected at random, or chosen to make three groups of three, which fits in well with the passage from Galatians. For example, there could be three berries, three citrus fruits and three 'orchard' fruits. This parallels with love, joy and peace, which are attitudes; kindness, goodness and faithfulness, which are actions; and patience, humility and self-control, which can be described as reactions.

It may be necessary to explain that God doesn't want us to sprout pieces of fruit on our bodies! However, just as we expect a plum tree to produce plums in the autumn, rather than any other kind of fruit, so God expects our lives to bear fruit for him in our thoughts, our actions and our words. Fruit takes a while to grow and develop, and we won't live perfect lives overnight. But it won't take long to see the evidence of growth once we become Christians. Jesus told us to abide in him, the true vine. Only by remaining attached to him, and allowing his life to fill ours, will we be able to produce this kind of fruit. Trying to live a good life is commendable, but impossible without the Holy Spirit within us. As you talk about each fruit, stick it (e.g. with velcro) to a volunteer's jumper, making sure the name written on it is the one you're referring to!

Pentecost – The Armour of God

The armour of God, as described by Paul in his letter to the Ephesians, is one of the most vivid pictures contained in the Bible. As with the fruits of the Spirit, it's best to let the picture speak for itself. Care should be exercised with this theme to emphasise the non-military and non-aggressive aspects of the Christian faith. It is sad that many folk have been given the wrong impression by the stereotyped evangelist who 'hits them' like a high-pressure salesman. Anything that might resemble manipulation of open and sensitive young minds will be viewed with suspicion. Fortunately, Paul himself condemned such tactics (see 1 Corinthians 2), and his use of the imagery of Roman armour is primarily 'defensive'. Children in particular are under great pressure to conform to the cynical, negative philosophy pumped at them by the media and society. They need the protection that God offers if their faith is to survive into adulthood and grow mature and strong.

HYMNS
Traditional
Father, hear the prayer we offer
Fight the good fight
Onward, Christian soldiers
Put thou thy trust in God
Soldiers of Christ arise
Stand up, stand up for Jesus
Who would true valour see
A safe stronghold
Christian soldiers, onward go
Lord of our life

Modern
Be bold, be strong
Let God arise
Rejoice, rejoice

Show your power, O Lord
Thanks be to God
The Lord has led forth his people
Jesus, we celebrate your victory
He that is in us
Hallelujah, for the Lord our God
God is our strength and refuge

READINGS
Judges 7:1-7,16-21/1 Samuel 17:32-50/ Isaiah 59:14-20/2 Corinthians 6:3-10/ Ephesians 6:10-20/1 Thessalonians 5:4-11/Matthew 26:47-56/Mark 9:14-29/ John 17:11-19.

CONFESSION
God our Father, we bring you in sorrow our sins and failings, asking you to forgive and restore us to yourself. We have lived in our own strength, ignoring the protection you offer, and the arrows of the evil one have wounded us. Forgive us and grant us the humility to see that only in you do we have a sure defence, and strength to stand firm for your kingdom. Amen.

God our heavenly Father forgive you your sins, and surround you with the protective armour of his Holy Spirit, that you may be alert and steadfast as you live for him. Amen.

PRAYER
Knowing that evil is already defeated, we come to our risen Saviour with our prayers and requests, saying,
Victorious Lord,
Protect us from the evil one.

When all around us deny the truth of the Gospel, and reject your claims, glorious Lord, may our faith be held together by the belt of truth.

Victorious Lord,
Protect us from the evil one.

When we are tempted to enter into conflict out of self-interest, may we remember that our feet are equipped to carry the gospel of peace.
Victorious Lord,
Protect us from the evil one.

When we are attacked by evil and feel in despair, may we hold up the shield of faith to repel all that would weaken our resolve to stand firm for you.
Victorious Lord,
Protect us from the evil one.

When our minds are assaulted by the pressures of the world around us, may the helmet of salvation resist all distractions and temptations to leave the way of Jesus.
Victorious Lord,
Protect us from the evil one.

When the enemy causes us to doubt your word and guiding hand, may we withstand him, not in our own strength but with the sword of the Spirit, which is God's word.

Victorious Lord,
**Protect us from the evil one
and help us to remain true to you,
unashamed of the Good News and
firm in our faith, for the sake of your
glory. Amen.**

SERMON IDEA
A 'straight' visual aid is needed for this picture, or it will lose its impact. Apparently it's possible to obtain from a fancy-dress hire shop, or some similar establishment, a Roman soldier's armour suitable for an average sized child. Alternatively you could persuade a good artist to draw you the appropriate gear in life size on stiff card, which you could then attach, piece by piece, to a volunteer (if you do this, check beforehand that it fits). Less striking, though quite adequate, would be overhead projector slides or drawings on a flip-chart.

As you discuss each piece of armour stress its spiritual meaning. All except one are for protection, not for attacking. The belt of truth holds everything together and was worn to give freedom of movement. Following Jesus brings us freedom, too. The breastplate of righteousness guards the heart, the source of love. The shoes of the gospel of peace give us a sure footing, enabling us to stand firm. When they move they bring peace from God, not conflict. The shield of faith was a hand-held defence against burning arrows, protecting the whole body, which could kneel behind it. The helmet of salvation protects our minds and thoughts, while the sword of the Spirit reminds us that we can only attack evil with the word of God and on his authority (cf Jesus when tempted). We follow our victorious Lord and live in the light of his victory.

Trinity

There are few harder concepts to convey to adults, let alone children, than that of God as a Trinity, three-in-one-and-one-in-three. Yet, at the same time, our faith depends on it. Excessive focus on just one person of the Trinity leads to a lack of balance and distorted theology. It's easy to be tempted to try to explain everything about our faith but God is beyond explanation. Rather than confuse listeners with theories, stress instead the importance of a faith that's rock-solid because it's balanced. It might also be helpful to underscore the unity of the Trinity which should be reflected in the life of the church.

HYMNS

Traditional

All my hope on God is founded
Father, Lord of all creation
Father of Heaven, whose love profound
Firmly I believe, and truly
Holy, holy, holy
My God, how wonderful thou art
I bind unto myself this day
Father most holy
May the grace of Christ our Saviour
Thou whose almighty word

Modern

Father we adore you
Father we love you
Holy, holy, holy is the Lord
Majesty
We believe in God the Father
Father in heaven
God of glory
O Lord our God
Jesus is Lord
Father God, we worship you

READINGS

Exodus 3:1-6/Psalm 9:1-l0/Isaiah 6:1-8/
Ephesians 1:3-14/Colossians l:9-14/
Revelation 5/Matthew 17:1-8
Mark 1:9-13/John 14:8-17.

CONFESSION

O Lord our God, enthroned on high,
filling the whole earth with your glory:
holy, holy, holy is your name.

Our eyes have seen the King, the Lord
almighty; but our lips are unclean.

We cry to you in our sinfulness to take
our guilt away, through Jesus Christ
our Lord. Amen.

May the Father forgive you by the
blood of the Son and strengthen you to
live in the power of the Spirit all your
days. Amen.

From *Church Family Worship*

PRAYER

God is three yet one and we come to
him with our prayers in awe at his
majesty, but responding to his invitation
to those who love him, saying,
Mighty God, have mercy on us,
And receive our prayer.

We come before our heavenly Father,
the king of kings, praying for his
world. Especially we pray for . . .
May your righteousness prevail and
your kingdom come.
Mighty God, have mercy on us,
And receive our prayer.

We come before our loving Saviour,
who died to redeem mankind, praying
for the Church, his forgiven people.
Especially we pray for . . .
May your love be demonstrated in our
lives, your care in our community and
your joy and peace in our relationships.
Mighty God, have mercy on us,
And receive our prayer.

We open our lives to the Holy Spirit, who reassures and strengthens us, praying that he will heal and comfort all who suffer. Especially we pray for . . . May your presence be with them in their needs and your hope sustain them in their time of darkness.

Mighty God, have mercy on us,
And receive our prayer. May our lives reflect the love of our Father in Heaven, the grace of our Lord Jesus Christ and the fellowship of the Holy Spirit for your sake. Amen.

SERMON IDEA

For this you will need a good camera tripod, ideally with a camera attached! If you're concerned about the safety of the equipment, use a gym mat or something similar so that it receives a soft landing. First of all show what happens when only one leg of the tripod is extended. Explain that if we only believe in God the Father, he will remain a distant person in heaven, uninterested in what's happening down here, or powerless to influence it. If we only believe in Jesus, he's nothing more than a good man. If we only believe in the Holy Spirit, we'll end up with just a few nice experiences that relate to nothing else. Then extend a second leg of the tripod. Better, but not at all stable. If we omit the Father we have no sense of God's greatness; if we omit Jesus, we can't relate him to our life on earth; if we leave out the Holy Spirit we have a very cerebral belief that has little effect on our lives and attitudes. We need all three to be balanced Christians. A tripod can stand firm on three legs, even in difficult circumstances (you could here demonstrate using a step or some other obstacle that requires one leg to be adjusted). All three legs work together to keep the camera still. The Father, Son and Holy Spirit are together in complete harmony. As they work together in unity, so we're called to reflect their life.

OTHER FESTIVALS

Although Christmas, Easter and Pentecost are the best-known festivals of the Church's year, there are many others which for the most part receive little attention. Mothering Sunday has been assaulted by the greetings card industry, and often draws people to church who otherwise rarely attend. It does give some opportunity to talk about families and how to live in them, but for many it's a painful day – the divorced, the bereaved, the single and lonely and so on. Great care is needed to avoid anyone feeling excluded or hurt. At the opposite end of the year comes Harvest, another crowd-puller, though more easily integrated into the life of the Church, because it emphasises that God's creation is for all of us to enjoy, not for a few to exploit. A useful alternative (or supplement) to Harvest is Rogation, another time to tackle the problems of ecology and 'green' issues.

Perhaps the most difficult is Remembrance Day. The generation of those who remember the Second World War is growing older, and while we've seen the Falklands and Gulf conflicts recently, they've neither affected so many people, nor been fought on our soil. Many children are, not unreasonably, pacifist by inclination, and will have grave doubts about what easily comes across as a celebration of militarism. However, there's a right sort of patriotism which isn't blind to its country's faults and doesn't glorify war: and it's good for every generation to be reminded of the horrors of warfare, especially with the weapons now at our disposal.

Saints' days can serve to emphasise a particular theme, and St Andrew and St Luke are included for that purpose. All Saints' Day is an excellent Christian counter to the Hallowe'en culture, and a good excuse for a celebration, too! All of them can add to the variety of worship that can be used in schools throughout the year.

Mothering Sunday

Most of us agree that mothers are wonderful things. They deserve a Sunday of being celebrated. How to do this meaningfully in a liturgical context is another question. In former times (when I was a small boy!) most Mums stayed at home. Even as recently as the early sixties some women were forced to leave their employment when they married, and remained tied to the home. There they did all the thankless tasks of washing, ironing, cleaning, cooking and caring and it made sense to set aside one day to thank and acknowledge them. These days many mothers have to work to pay the mortgage or rent – if Dad's unemployed Mum may be the breadwinner. Women also have very different expectations in terms of career and status from their counterparts of fifty years ago.

Many churches use Mothering Sunday to emphasise a stable family life – not that we thank mothers any less, because many of them add part or full-time employment to all the household duties. The rise in the number of divorces and broken families is another changed factor in our society. When all of them are mixed together, they produce an odd cocktail. For some, even in a school service, this is a painful day. Bereavement, divorce or separation, or other family distress can easily cause pain instead of contentment. Mothering Sunday must minister to the needs of those who find it a day they would rather forget. However, that shouldn't be at the expense of thanking mothers and affirming them. In a society where the more extreme elements view motherhood as a social evil and the family as a man-made prison, we can be bold in saying that they're God's gifts to us.

HYMNS
Traditional
Now thank we all our God
For the beauty of the earth
Great is thy faithfulness
Morning has broken
Jesus, good above all other
Tell out, my soul
Glorious things of thee are spoken
Help us to help each other, Lord

Modern
Jesus put this song into our hearts
The King is among us
Let us sing to the God of salvation
Let there be love
Bind us together
Jesus, stand among us
Jehovah Jireh, my provider
Make me a channel of your peace

READINGS
Exodus 2:1-10/1 Samuel 1:1-20/ Ephesians 5:21-6:4/Colossians 3:15-4:11/ Peter 3:1-7/Mark 10:13-16/John 2: 1-11/John 19:25-28.

CONFESSION
O God, the Father of us all, we come to you in sorrow,
for we have often failed you.
Lord, forgive us, and help us to obey.

You have taught us: 'Honour your father and mother, that it may go well with you and that you enjoy long life on the earth.'
We have often failed you.
Lord, forgive us, and help us to obey.

You have taught us as children: 'Obey your parents in the Lord, for this is right.'
We have often failed you.
Lord, forgive us, and help us to obey.

You have taught us as fathers: 'Do not exasperate your children; instead, bring them up in the training and instruction of the Lord.'
We have often failed you.
Lord, forgive us, and help us to obey.

You have taught us as mothers to live with sincere faith and bring our children to Christ.
We have often failed you.
Lord, forgive us, and help us to obey

You have taught us as the Christian family: 'Submit to one another out of reverence for Christ.'
We have often failed you.
Lord, forgive us, and help us to obey.
Father, help us all to hear your word, and to obey it; for Jesus' sake. Amen.

This is based on Ephesians 5 and 6 and is adapted from *Church Family Worship*.

PRAYERS

We join together in thanksgiving and praise to our eternal Father as we say,
Father in Heaven, receive our praise,
And hear your children's prayer.

We thank you, loving Father, for your gift of love and family life . . . Help us to live with our loved ones in an atmosphere of peace and joy, where your love reigns and your will is done.
Father in Heaven, receive our praise
And hear your children's prayer.

We thank you, mighty Lord, that your love reaches out to everyone . . . Help those who have authority in this world to follow the ways of peace and righteousness.
Father in Heaven, receive our prayer,
And hear your children's prayer.

We thank you, gracious Spirit, that your presence is within us day by day . . . Help us to live in his strength, which enables us to serve as you call us.
Father in Heaven, receive our praise,
And hear your children's prayer.

We thank you, caring Saviour, that you have compassion on all who suffer in mind or body . . . Help us to show your care to all in need, and draw them into your presence
Father in Heaven, receive our praise,
And hear your children's prayer. Make us one as you are one, and build us up as your family, brothers and sisters in our Lord Jesus Christ, Amen.

SERMON IDEA

Mothers do many things for their children. Providing food, clean clothes, and limitless caring are just a few. If competent mimers available, they could effectively mime some of these tasks. What do Mums expect in return from their offspring? They can reasonably expect obedience (you could write the word on a flip-chart or OHP). It makes their life so much easier if we do as we're told. God's people are a family, too, and he expects obedience of them.

A vital part of living together as his family involves doing his will and obeying him. Stress that most mothers don't expect unreasonable things of their children, so God does not expect unreasonable things of his. Suggest a few areas for obedience to mothers (going to bed, for example or doing music practice), then invite suggestions about how God wants us to obey him. Mums also like us to be helpful (again, write up the word if you can, and invite more ideas about how we can help, e.g. by preparing food or tidyinf the bedroon). God wants us to help willingly, by encouraging and supporting one another. Just as we take responsibility in a family, to play our part in it, so as Christians we must play our part in God's family. We must also care for our mothers. They need to be cared for as much as anyone else. God asks us to care for each other, most of all in times of need. As we do so, we reflect God's love to those around us.

Rogation

Rogationtide has its roots in the countryside and rural community. As a result its original significance may be lost to many children whose knowledge of country life is limited. Even in rural Surrey, where I'm writing this, there's little in the way of a farming community around us. The majority of the residents of our parish are employed in towns or cities, and understand country life in those terms.

Transportation of goods from other parts of the world also means that food which used to be available only seasonally is now to hand most of the time in our supermarkets. But although in the west we enjoy a surfeit of good food and resources in plenty, most of the world's population isn't so fortunate. Rogation is therefore a good time to thank God for all his goodness in creation, and to remember the needs of seventy-five per cent of the inhabitants of this planet. Better still, the teaching could be allied to a project to provide practical help to a third world country, perhaps using Tear Fund, Cafod, Oxfam or one of the other big relief agencies.

HYMNS

Traditional
All things bright and beautiful
Immortal, invisible
Let us with a gladsome mind
Praise the Lord, ye heavens
O worship the King

Modern
Think of a world without any flowers
Morning has broken
Angels praise him
Thou art worthy
Praise him on the trumpet

Many of the Harvest hymns may also be suitable.

READINGS

Genesis 2:4-9 Deuteronomy 8:1-10/ Psalm 148/2 Thessalonians 3:6-13/ Revelation 21:1-7/Matthew 6:1-15/ Luke 11:5-13/John 6: 1-13.

CONFESSION

Creator God, we have misused the world you made through carelessness, selfishness and wastefulness. We confess that we have given little thought to our environment, our fellow human beings in need, or your Kingdom. Forgive us we pray, and deliver us from complacency, that we may rejoice in your provision and use it for the good of mankind, for the sake of your Son Christ our Lord, Amen.

God our heavenly Father cleanse you from all sin, fill you with his love and set you free to serve him, for his name's sake. Amen.

PRAYER

Rejoicing in all that our loving Father has provided us with, we bring before him our requests and prayers, saying,
Generous God, accept our thanks,
And receive our prayers.

Thank you, heavenly Father, for creating our world and allowing us to enjoy all you have made. Help us, we pray to treat it responsibly and enable everyone to benefit from it.
Generous God, accept our thanks,
And receive our prayers.

Thank you, heavenly Father, for providing our daily food, our homes and all that we need. Help us, we pray, to show our gratitude by sharing what you have given us with those in need.
Generous God, accept our thanks,
And receive our prayers.

Thank you, heavenly Father, for our daily work, which enables us to share in your creative work. Help us, we pray, to apply ourselves to our tasks and do them as for you.
Generous God, accept our thanks,
And receive our prayers.

Thank you, heavenly Father, for families and friends to share our lives with. Help us, we pray, to show your love in all our relationships and pursue the ways of peace.
Generous God, accept our thanks,
And receive our prayers.

Thank you, heavenly Father, for your love and care, which transforms our lives. Help us, we pray, to bring your Good News to all who are suffering or in need.
Generous God, accept our thanks,
And receive our prayers, for the sake of your Son Jesus Christ. Amen.

SERMON IDEA

This talk is based on the feeding of the five thousand. To make a real impression, set up a table in front of the congregation, and prepare it as for a picnic. (A cloth on the ground may be more authentic, but it's unlikely to be very visible.) Invite four volunteers to sit around it and then lay out the food. The more exotic the repast looks, the better. Sandwiches (you could tell them the filling is smoked salmon or caviar), crisps, salads, fruit, cakes and a bottle of chilled wine or champagne all look very impressive. When all is prepared start by explaining that we in the West are very fortunate to enjoy such good food. For the majority of the world's population such things are undreamt of luxury. One by one remove all the choice items, and replace them with a packet of rice (to last a week) and a glass of water (only one a day). Most of the congregation will have seen pictures of poverty and starvation in the third world, so build on that to make the point that we enjoy a great deal at the expense of the poor. We may want to do something to help, but it seems so little and ineffective it just isn't worth it. Then tell the story of the feeding of the five thousand, emphasising how small (and probably squishy!) the small boy's packed lunch was. But by offering it to Jesus it was turned into a feast for thousands. If we offer what we can to God to use, however little it may seem to us, we'll be amazed at what he can do with it.

Harvest

Harvest, like Rogation, is a festival concerned with Creation and God's goodness to us. Unlike Rogation, it's a festival which draws many people into church who would otherwise not come. Part of the appeal is practical service. Most celebrations of Harvest involve the congregation presenting produce which is then distributed among the elderly and needy. That's great as an idea, but it needs to be well thought through – many perishable food stuffs start to go off before they can be delivered, and most homes for the elderly plan their menus well in advance. Another potential danger is that, having 'done their bit' some folk will see the harvest basket as the sum total of their Christian charity.

The service should emphasise that it's our gratitude to God which should motivate our giving and serving. He doesn't just want the fruits of our larders and freezers, but the fruits of our lives. This is particularly relevant because most children are aware that fruit and vegetables can be bought in the supermarket at any time of year. Perhaps a specific project of Christian giving could be launched at a Harvest service, with details given the following year of how much has been raised.

HYMNS

Traditional
We plough the fields and scatter
Come, ye thankful people come
All things bright and beautiful
All creatures of our God and King
O Lord my God
For the beauty of the earth
For the fruits of his creation
To thee, O Lord
Fill your hearts with joy
Praise and thanksgiving

Modern
Fear not, rejoice and be glad
Jehovah Jireh
Jesus is Lord
All earth was dark
Ah, Lord God
God is good
O the valleys shall ring
O Lord our God, how majestic is your name
Praise God from whom all blessings flow
Stand up, clap hands

READINGS

Genesis 1:1-3,26-31/Deuteronomy 26: 1-12/Psalms 65 and 67/Acts 14:13-17/ 2 Corinthians 9:6-15/1 Timothy 6:6-10, 17-19/Matthew 13:1-9 (or 23)/ Luke 12:16-21 (or 31)/John 6:27-35.

CONFESSION

We confess our sins to our heavenly Father, saying,
Merciful God,
Forgive our sins.

We confess our ingratitude for all that you have provided us with, and ask you to pardon our self-reliance.
Merciful God,
Forgive our sins.

We confess our thoughtlessness in ignoring the plight of the starving and despairing, and ask you to forgive our selfish attitudes.
Merciful God,
Forgive our sins.

We confess our carelessness in not treating the world as your creation or acting as good stewards of your gifts, and ask you to deliver us from self-centredness
Merciful God,
Forgive our sins.
We confess our unwillingness to

acknowledge you as the source and giver of all we have, and ask you to cleanse us from self-will.

Merciful God,
Forgive our sins and fill our hearts with gratitude to you and concern for the needs of all people through Christ our Lord. Amen.

PRAYER

Thanking God for all blessings,
we stand before him as our heavenly Father, saying,

Father we thank you,
And praise your name.

For the beauty of hills and mountains, for the richness of farmland and forest, and for the bustle of city and town,

Father we thank you,
And praise your name.

For the peace of the river, the power of the sea and the fish that live in them,

Father we thank you,
And praise your name.

For the produce of fields and orchards, for rain and water to sustain growth, and for all we have to eat and drink,

Father we thank you,
And praise your name.

For health and strength to enjoy this world, to work in it and to husband its resources,

Father we thank you,
And praise your name.

For all who work on the land or on the sea, in factory or office, in shop or home,

Father we thank you,
And praise your name.

For those who work in caring for the sick, elderly, handicapped and dying, and all whose work meets our needs,

Father we thank you,

And praise your name. May we join with all creation in declaring your glory, revealed to us all in Jesus Christ our Lord. Amen.

SERMON IDEA

You'll need two smallish plants in pots, one healthy and vigorous, the other rather sad-looking and tatty. Two apples or oranges can also be used, one shiny and enticing, the other shrivelled and nasty. Jesus' parable about the sower provides the Biblical foundation.

Start by the point that growth is the primary evidence for life. If a plant stops growing it's dead! Explain that this is true of spiritual life. The seed of God's word falls on our lives, but it doesn't always grow very well. Sometimes it doesn't seem to grow at all. (You could throw some seed on the floor, and ask if it's likely to grow.) But many seeds germinate. Then (bring out the poor-looking plant) something goes wrong. Sometimes it's not got enough soil or the right conditions to grow properly. Even though we listen to God's word, it doesn't grow properly, because so many things prevent it (such as pressures of work, distractions of the media, and the opinions of others). God doesn't want us to be like that plant. Instead (produce the healthy one) he wants us to grow strong in him by putting our roots deep in the soil of his love. Jesus said that if we are like seed planted in good soil we'll not only grow but bear fruit. Healthy plants produce beautiful flowers or a good crop (show the shiny fruit). As we live in God, and allow Jesus' risen life to fill us (cf John 15) our lives will bear the evidence of that. But fruit must be used, if left it goes like this (bring out the shrivelled one). God enables us to bear fruit so that others can benefit.

All Saints

All Saints' Day is becoming increasingly popular. Many Christians, concerned at the rise in Satanism and Occult practises, are unhappy about the traditional celebration of Hallowe'en. An All Saints Eve service is an excellent antidote to witches and pumpkins, which may seem harmless in themselves, but could lead to children not recognising the reality of evil. The first such service to be held in Guildford Cathedral attracted so many people that several hundred were unable to get into the building.

Another good reason for celebrating All Saints' is that we live in a very individualistic culture, which affects our churches. It's good to be reminded that God created us for himself and one another. We're made to live in community. Instead of focusing on evil (even in a light-hearted way) it's surely better to set our minds on what's good and right, and give thanks for the lives of those who have brought the love of God to the world and to our lives.

If the weather allows, a firework party is a splendid culmination to the proceedings, though any sort of party emphasises that the Christian life isn't dull or dreary – God wants us to laugh and enjoy ourselves.

HYMNS

Traditional
Disposer supreme
For all the saints
For all thy saints, O Lord
Soldiers who are Christ's below
You servants of God
Look, you saints, the sight is glorious
Come, let us join our cheerful songs
Let saints on earth in concert sing
Jerusalem, my happy home
Through the night of doubt and sorrow

Modern
We are a chosen people
We'll walk the land
Jesus put this song into our hearts
From the sun's rising
I will build my church
As we are gathered
O Lord, most holy God
For I'm building a people of power
Lord for the years
Bind us together

READINGS

Psalm 145/Isaiah 65:17-25/Jeremiah 31:31-34/Ephesians 1:15-23/Hebrews 12:18-24/Revelation 19:5-10/ Matthew 13:1-9/5:1-12/Luke 6:20-23.

CONFESSION

Almighty God, you have called us to be members of your glorious Kingdom of light, yet we have forgotten that we are citizens of Heaven, and children of Heaven's King. Our eyes have been fixed on the things of this earth, and we have failed to see you in your glory. In your mercy forgive us for all our sins, and raise us together with Christ to the heavenly places where you dwell for ever, for your name's sake. Amen.

God our merciful Father, who forgives all who truly repent, cleanse you from every kind of wrong and set your minds on the things which are above for the sake of his Son, our Saviour Jesus Christ. Amen.

PRAYER

As citizens of God's eternal Kingdom we come before him, saying,
accept our praise,
Heavenly King,
And receive your people's prayer.

We rejoice with all God's saints in the victory of Christ over all that is evil, and over the power of death. May our lives reflect what is right and good, and show forth the joys of our eternal home.
Accept our praise, Heavenly King,
And receive your people's prayer.

We remember with gratitude all whose lives and words have led us to Christ and awakened our faith. May we in our turn live and speak so that other people are drawn to your love.
Accept our praise, Heavenly King,
And receive your people's prayer.

We rejoice that in the face of persecution and death your servants have remained steadfast in faith and witness. May we be strengthened by their example and made bold to declare your truth.
Accept our praise, Heavenly King,
And receive your people's prayer.

We remember all who have served you faithfully, both those whose names are well-known and those who are known only to you. May we too serve you like them, for no reward other than hearing your 'Well done, good and faithful servant'.
Accept our praise, Heavenly King,
And receive your people's prayer. Go with us on our earthly pilgrimage and bring us at last to the joy of your everlasting Kingdom, through Jesus Christ our Lord. Amen.

Sermon Idea

There are several interlinking themes to All Saints' Day – Heaven, those who've achieved great things for God, encouragement to those on their pilgrimage, and so on. Overcoming obstacles and distractions is a fundamental part of our Christian journey.

One idea would be to have an obstacle race, starting at the font (if it's portable put it at the back of the church) and progressing over such barricades as materialism (a pile of possessions would fit the bill well) disappointment, sadness, doubt and work pressures (you could make up many more to suit your own situation or points you want to make, e.g. poverty, illness, unemployment, old age). Show how the 'great' saints have overcome all these with God's help, ideally using stories.

An alternative in a building that won't take a 'race' is to draw up a board game either on OHP acetates or flip chart pages, using a dice throw to make progress towards 'Heaven'. Either offers scope for involving the congregation. Finish by encouraging them not to give up when things get tough, and to keep their heavenly home in view all the time.

Remembrance

Remembrance is a liturgical minefield! There are more prize corns waiting to be trodden on here than almost anywhere else in the Church's year, and although to many children it may seem an outdated ritual we'd be better off without, there are many schools which still want to highlight it. It's also still well to the fore in our national consciousness, and likely to remain there. Accordingly, it's best to make the most of the opportunity it presents.

There are strong points to be made about war, but that can easily degenerate into glorifying aggression, or at the opposite end of the scale a pacifist tract. James' letter provides a useful way in – where does conflict and strife originate? (see James 4:12). Children generate plenty of squabbles, albeit at varying levels of sophistication, and there's much potential for teaching about relationships, both on an individual and an international basis.

Hymns

Traditional
All people that on earth do dwell
Through the night of doubt and sorrow
O God our help in ages past
Lead us, Heavenly Father, lead us
Through all the changing scenes
Lord of our life
God moves in a mysterious way
Oft in danger, oft in woe

Modern
Rejoice, rejoice
Safe in the shadow of the Lord
Thanks be to God who gives us the victory
God is our strength and refuge
Living under the shadow of his wing
I lift my eyes to the quiet hills
My peace I give unto you
Make me a channel of your peace

Readings
Psalm 46/Isaiah 2:1-5/Micah 4:1-5/ Romans 8:31-end/1 Corinthians 15:50-end/James 4:1-12/Matthew 5:43-48/ Mark 12:28-34/John 15:9-17.

Confession
Let us return to the Lord our God
and say to him:

Father, we have sinned against heaven and against you. We are not worthy to be called your children. We turn to you again. Have mercy on us; bring us back to yourself as those who once were dead but now have life through Christ our Lord. Amen

My God our Father forgive you your sins, and bring you to the fellowship of his table, with his saints for ever.
Amen.

From *Patterns for Worship*

Prayer
We bring the needs of the world
and our own needs before God, saying,
Lord of peace,
Help us to trust you more.

When the problems of the world fill us with dismay, when violence and hatred are increasing, we ask that your peace will reign over all the earth. In particular we pray for . . .
Lord of Peace,
Help us to trust you more.

When the problems in our community affect our lives, when conflicts among our friends urge us to take sides, we ask that your peace will reign, bringing reconciliation and hope. In particular we pray for . . .
Lord of peace,
Help us to trust you more.

When we are tempted to defend our own corner, to promote our own interests without considering our friends and families, we ask that your peace will reign in our homes. In particular we pray for . . .

Lord of peace,
Help us to trust you more.

When our hearts are full of turmoil, when our lives are torn apart by tension and uncertainty, we ask that your peace will reign in our hearts. In particular we pray for . . .

Lord of peace,
Help us to trust you more and to allow your peace to be the final arbiter in all we do, through Christ our Lord, who died to bring us peace. Amen.

Sermon Idea

There may be times when war is just, or conflict justified, but no-one is likely to say that warfare or antagonism are in themselves good or constructive things. Peace is an excellent Remembrance theme, therefore.

There are different ways in which we use the word 'peace'. Peace can be nothing more than an absence of noise (easily demonstrated with a cassette recorder at full volume!) or an absence of conflict. The fact that two people aren't physically fighting doesn't mean they're getting on well – there may be an underlying issue which will break out in conflict unless tackled. This can be demonstrated by prearranging a scrap, though make sure the volunteers are well briefed beforehand not to get out of hand – they must shake hands as soon as you intervene! An alternative is to use a well-drawn cartoon picture. Peace can also be an absence of busyness and activity (a moment of silence will reinforce this).

In the Bible peace means something more, however. 'Shalom', a word the children may be familiar with from a well-known song, is a state of harmony and well-being. It isn't something we create but a gift from God. Jesus died so that we could once again enjoy a relationship of love with our heavenly Father, and when we trust in him, his peace comes into our lives. It means knowing our sins are forgiven, that we're loved and treasured by God, that whatever happens around us, nothing can take us away from his love. When that love is within us, it changes all our relationships and enables us to be peacemakers instead of causing conflict. If everyone lived in the light of God's peace, our world would be a very different place.

St Luke

Saints' days probably strike most children as the ultimate in ecclesiastical ennui! To be fair, many of them aren't exactly riveting from a child's viewpoint, but one or two are very helpful in exploring a particular theme. The rise in interest in the Christian healing ministry, and the generally high profile given in the media to health issues means that there's an important area of Christian teaching to handle. School services are not the place for a healing session with laying on of hands. However, many people will be aware of others who have been inexplicably healed, or apparently haven't received healing despite being prayed for.

The Church, as it follows the example and teaching of Jesus, has a clear duty to minister healing in his name, but it's vital to avoid giving the impression that this is a superior and faster alternative to the NHS, or that it's an activity indulged in by a few nutcases. There's much misunderstanding in this area which needs clarification. Dr Luke gives the opportunity to do this, and to give thanks for the work of medical and nursing staff. It can also help to make sense of praying for the sick and dying.

HYMNS
Traditional
Praise, my soul, the King of Heaven
At even, 'ere the sun was set
Healing God, almighty Father
Lord I was blind
O for a thousand tongues to sing
Thou Lord hast given thyself
And can it be
God is love, let Heaven adore him

Modern
Praise you Lord, for the wonder of
  your healing.
Be still and know

Give thanks with a grateful heart
The price is paid
Peter and John went to pray
Jesus you are changing me
Lord have mercy upon us
Jesus you are the radiance

READINGS
1 Kings 17:17-24 / Psalm 103:1-12 (or end) / Isaiah 38:1-8, 21-22 / Acts 3:1-16 / 1 Corinthians 12:7-11 / James 5:13-16 / Mark 2:1-12 / 5:1-20 / Luke 9:40-56 / John 5:1-15 / 9:1-11, 35-41.

CONFESSION
Come let us return to the Lord and say:

Lord our God, in our sin we have avoided your call. Our love for you is like the mist, disappearing in the heat of the sun. Have mercy on us. Bind up our wounds, and bring us back to the foot of the cross, through Jesus Christ our Lord. Amen.

May the God of love bring *you* back to himself, forgive *you your* sins, and assure *you* of his eternal love in Jesus Christ our Lord. Amen.

From *Patterns for Worship*

PRAYER
Lord Jesus, you showed compassion to all who came to you in sickness or distress. Hear our prayers for those who need your healing touch today.
Loving Lord Jesus,
Heal us we pray.

We pray for the needs of our world. Comfort and heal all who suffer from hunger, poverty, fear or oppression. Especially . . .
Loving Lord Jesus,
Heal your world, we pray.

We pray for our divided church. Heal our conflicts and help us to live in the unity you died to bring. Especially . . .
Loving Lord Jesus,
Heal your church, we pray.

We pray for our families and friends. Heal our broken relationships and breathe your peace into our lives. Especially . . .
Loving Lord Jesus,
Heal our homes, we pray.

We pray for those we know who are ill or suffering in any way. Heal them and meet their deepest needs. Especially . . .
Loving Lord Jesus,
Heal our friends we pray.

We pray for ourselves. Heal our fears and sadness and fill our hearts with your unending joy.
Loving Lord Jesus,
Heal us all and help us to live in your strength alone, to your praise and glory. Amen.

SERMON IDEA

It's rather difficult to use much volunteer help with this theme. The best option is to ask a skilled artist to draw some OHP slides or flip-charts to illustrate the points. Healing doesn't just mean an instant cure – much unnecessary distress has been caused by conveying this idea. Sometimes physical ailments are healed in this way, but many will ask 'What about the ones who aren't healed?' The Hebrew word 'shalom' means 'wholeness', and the healing of Jesus brought wholeness to many lives. When he healed those who were blind or crippled, he also enabled them to be accepted in society and live a normal life.

The first OHP could be of medication or a First-Aid kit. God has given us the means to deal with many illnesses or injuries and we should make use of them. The next OHP could be of a surgeon or operating theatre, showing how God has given skill to enable doctors to diagnose what's wrong and put it right. Emphasise that this healing is just as much God-given as the more spectacular variety! A picture of a sad face or person next will help to introduce the idea that God can heal our minds and emotions as well as our bodies. Often we fail to recognise our need of this 'inner healing', because its symptoms are less obvious.

A further picture of two people quarrelling will make the point that relationships often need Jesus' healing power, too. With care you could also explain that some people can't help the way they behave, and may need a kind of spiritual healing of the root cause of their problems. Finally stress how Jesus always dealt with the root of the problem (e.g. the man lowered through the roof, or the woman at the well), by forgiving sin. However, don't imply that all physical illness is due to specific personal sin.

St Andrew

Evangelism is a word that strikes fear into the hearts. It conjures up images of emotional excesses or simulated ecstasy, and for many is associated with dubious methods of fund-raising and unscrupulous manipulators of the media. That's a shame, because true evangelism has nothing to do with handkerchieves with a blessing in each corner, nor does it require anyone to throw their marbles down the aisle!

Andrew is often used as a case-study in evangelism, because he did nothing except tell his brother the good news about Jesus. Unfortunately the Church tends to give the impression that enthusiasm and faith should never be mixed together, but nothing draws people and fires them up like enthusiasm. The Church is also rather individualistic in culture, so religious belief and practise can become an unhealthily personal thing.

Sharing the good news of Jesus with others is neither individualistic nor personal, however. It forces us to take account of others' needs and concerns and prevents us from being self-centred in our faith. Most children will respond to any kind of enthusiasm. So long as they aren't being manipulated or led up the garden path, their minds will remain open and free of adult 'clutter'. Incidentally, there's no quicker way to grow in understanding the Christian faith than by sharing it with others.

HYMNS

Traditional
We have a gospel to proclaim
Ye servants of God
We have heard a joyful sound
Lift high the Cross
Go forth and tell
Lord, speak to me
Let all the world
Forth in the peace of Christ

Modern
We are marching
We shall stand
Send me out from here, Lord
From the sun's rising
One shall tell another
So I've made up my mind
God's Spirit is in my heart
How lovely on the mountains

READINGS
Psalm 86:8-17/Isaiah 45:18-end/ Zechariah 8:20-end/Romans 10:12-18/ Galatians 3:26-4:7/Ephesians 2:14-end/ Matthew 4:12-20/28:16-20/ John 1:35-42.

CONFESSION
Lord Jesus, you commanded your disciples to proclaim your good news to all people, but we have failed to bear witness to your saving love, either with our lips or our lives. We are sorry, and ask you to forgive our reluctance to share the gospel. Fill our hearts with the joy of your risen presence, and our wills with the desire to make your name known throughout the world, through Christ our Lord. Amen.

God our loving Father have mercy on you, forgive all your sins and pardon your reluctance so that you may be free to declare his praises and live for his glory. Amen.

PRAYER
We pray for the coming of God's kingdom, saying,
Father, by your Spirit,
Bring in your kingdom.

You came in Jesus to bring good news
to the poor, sight to the blind, freedom
to the captives, and salvation to all
people; anoint us with your Spirit;
rouse us to work in your name.
Father, by your Spirit,
Bring in your kingdom.

Send us to bring help to the poor and
freedom to the oppressed.
Father, by your Spirit,
Bring in your kingdom.

Send us to tell the world the good news
of your healing love.
Father, by your Spirit,
Bring in your kingdom.

Send us to those who mourn, to bring
joy and gladness instead of grief.
Father, by your Spirit,
Bring in your kingdom.

Send us to proclaim that the time is
here for you to save your people.
Father, by your Spirit,
Bring in your kingdom.

Lord of the Church
**Hear our prayer, and make us one in
heart and mind to serve you in Christ
our Lord. Amen.**

From *Patterns for Worship*

SERMON IDEA

Since evangelism involves sharing the
good news about Jesus, an effective
idea is to ask two volunteers to read
some 'news' items as though it were a
TV bulletin. The first two or three
could be fairly humorous in style (the
Two Ronnies produced some wonderful examples of this, though
regrettably some of their material is too

risqué by far). Thereafter, you could
incorporate some genuine headlines
and ask whether they're good or bad
news. Many are ambiguous – writing
this in a general election year, I am
reminded that the result of that was
either good or bad news, depending on
your views! The material will need to
be adjusted to the particular age-group
involved.

In human terms good news is
usually relative. Point out that the
good news of Jesus isn't like that. It's
good news for all people, unlike a
football victory (which means defeat
for someone else) or even a tax cut
(which won't benefit every one). It's
also good news for all time. Most
human news is temporary. It soon
changes for one reason or another. Tax
cuts become increases; one war finishes
and another breaks out; a murderer is
found guilty, but there's another one
not yet caught. It's also good news for
all places. The gospel is universal in its
application. Anyone can hear the good
news and respond to it, wherever they
live, however much or little money
they may have, whatever the colour of
their skin.

Finally, write out some of the
passion narrative as banner headlines
on large pieces of card. Show how the
arrest, trial and crucifixion of Jesus
looked like totally bad news, but was
in reality the best news the world has
ever had. Forgiveness, freedom, new
life, hope . . . all are ours in Christ if we
trust in him.

THE CHURCH

In the late 1980s I was asked to take a series of assemblies for a well-known boys' school. I chose to speak about the Church and started with a brief survey. About nine hundred pupils were present, and I asked first what they found most difficult about the Christian faith – was it intellectually beyond the pale or totally irrational? A small handful put their hands up at this juncture (brave indeed, since the Headmaster was on the platform with me!). Next I enquired as to how many found the problem of reconciling suffering with a God of love the biggest stumbling block to faith. Around twenty per cent assented to this. Finally, I asked what proportion of the assembled youth thought the Church was the real hindrance to accepting the Christian faith. You've probably guessed – at least half the hands went up! I can't say I found it a huge surprise. For many of them the Church was at best a marginal institution, possibly doing a bit of good here and there but of little relevance to modern society.

It's amazing how many folk have had a bad experience of the Church somewhere along the line. A vicar who seemed uncaring, an organisation that appeared inflexible, a community that came across as judgemental . . . Most clergy have been told that the reason Mr Jones doesn't come to church is because it's full of hypocrites. A bishop was once told this by a member of the aristocracy whose churchgoing had lapsed many years earlier. The bishop, with great presence of mind, responded that the man should try it again as he'd probably feel quite at home!

The following services are built around some of the pictures of God's people found in the Bible. They are not likely to do much about deep-rooted prejudice, but may be of help in preventing the prejudice from taking root so easily in young and impressionable minds. All of them are vivid pictures, and lend themselves well to the school setting. They aren't tied to a particular time of year and can stand on their own, as well as in a series.

God's Family

There are few bigger 'cringe factors' than hearing someone describe their part of the community as 'a great big happy family'! There's no such thing as a completely happy family. Disputes flare up between husband and wife, parent and child, brother and sister. It doesn't improve much with age, either. The elderly and their grown-up children are just as prone to falling out with each other. It's essential that in describing the Church as God's family we don't put on rose-tinted spectacles and pretend there are no problems.

The expression 'family of God' is only used once in the Bible (1 Peter 4:17), though the 'household of God' (l Timothy 3:15) is very similar. There's also a wonderful passage in Ephesians 3:14-21 which makes the same point. However, it isn't laboured. The frequent references to fellow Christians as brothers and sisters, and both Paul and John's descriptions of their readers as 'dear children' imply that the relationships among Christian people are similar to those in a human family. That means occasional disagreements and rows; it means we grow and mature together in Christ; it means an end to spiritual individualism, a new emphasis on cooperation and mutual love and care. This is a very good picture of the Church to use with children, as most of them will have some concept of the family and what it ought to be, even if theirs doesn't live up to it.

HYMNS

Traditional
Our father, by whose name
Lord of all hopefulness
I come with joy to meet my Lord
Jesus where'er thy people meet
For the beauty of the earth
O Holy Spirit, Lord of Grace

Now thank we all our God
What a friend we have in Jesus
Let saints on earth together sing
Blessed be the tie that binds

Modern
Bind us together
Father I place into your hands
A new commandment I give unto you
Let there be love shared among us
Jesus, stand among us
Jesus put this song into our hearts
There's a quiet understanding
As we are gathered
For I'm building a people of power
Living under the shadow of his wing

READINGS

Exodus 19:1-9/Psalm 37:27-40/Hosea 11/Ephesians 3:14-21/Philippians 2:1-11/1 John 3:16-20/Matthew 18:15-20/21-35/20:20-28.

CONFESSION

Heavenly Father, you have called us to be part of your family, but we have often acted as though it meant nothing. Forgive us for the times when we have behaved selfishly, thinking of our own interests and caring little for the needs of others. Create in us the mind which was in Christ Jesus, that we may follow the way of our Servant King. Amen.

Almighty God, who has mercy on all who turn to him with contrite hearts, pardon you from all self-will and pride and deliver you from unloving attitudes, that you may be free to love him with all your heart and your neighbour as yourself, through Christ our Lord. Amen.

PRAYER

We pray for the family of God's Church and for all human relationships as we say,

Loving Father,
Receive our prayer.

We pray for the household of faith, your spiritual family here on earth. In particular we ask . . . Grant your people the strength to live in the unity your Son gave his life to win.
Loving Father,
Receive our prayer.

We pray for the whole family of those who live on this earth. In particular we ask . . . Grant the nations courage to pursue the paths of peace and righteousness.
Loving Father,
Receive our prayer.

We pray for all human families and households, especially those of which we are part. In particular we ask . . . Grant us peace and humility in all our relationships.
Loving Father,
Receive our prayer.

We pray for those who have no human family, and for all who are lonely or afraid. In particular we ask . . . Grant them your comfort and draw them into the circle of your family.
Loving Father,
Receive our prayer, and surround us, with your love for the sake of your Son, Jesus Christ, who died to make us one. Amen.

SERMON IDEA
There are plenty of analogies you could use from human families to illustrate truths about the family of God, but too many could cause confusion! The following four points fit together and can be illustrated using OHP slides or a flip-chart, with suitable cartoons for the images described. It's worth preparing these visual aids well as they can be used again. Make sure they're big enough to be visible from the back row! Start by stating that we're born into a human family. As you show a picture of a small baby, point out that we become part of God's family by being born again (a sadly misused and misunderstood phrase). It's the beginning of our spiritual life.

Show a picture of a child, playing or learning in school. When a baby's born it starts to grow at once. God gives us human families to grow up safely in. In the same way, Christians grow up spiritually in the Church, becoming stronger in their faith and learning more about God each day.

The next illustration should be of children squabbling. It's in our families that we learn to live together peacefully. As we live with our parents, our brothers and sisters, and then the wider circle of family and friends, we build up relationships. We learn that some forms of behaviour annoy or upset people, that we make friends by caring about others, and that quarrels have to be sorted out before friendship can resume. As Christians we have to grow together in the Church, finding out about our relationships with one another (often the hard way!) and sorting out our differences.

Finally, show a picture of adults helping small children. As we grow up to adulthood we have to take responsibility ourselves within the family. That means not just sorting out our own lives but also helping others who haven't progressed as far in the journey of life. Growing into spiritual maturity implies that we care for those starting out in the Christian faith, or finding it difficult. We aren't perfect but God wants us to be part of his family so that we become mature in him, ready for whatever he calls us to do.

God's Building

The concept of the Church as 'God's building' is, like that of his Family, one which permeates the whole New Testament, though with few direct references. It's another splendidly graphic image, lending itself to visual aids. Children for the most part will be familiar with Lego bricks or similar construction toys, and it's useful to build on such knowledge. Both Paul and Peter use this image in the context of Christian unity. It's very significant that all the New Testament pictures of the Church involve working together and being part of the overall pattern of God's work. The Church two thousand years ago clearly wasn't so different from ours.

Hymns

Traditional

Christ is made the sure foundation
The Church's one foundation
Christ is our corner-stone
Glorious things of thee are spoken
O Christ, the great foundation
A safe stronghold
Thy hand, O God, has guided
Angel voices ever singing

Modern

For I'm building a people of power
God is building a house
I will build my church
We have come into his house
We will stand with our feet on a rock
In our church Lord, be glorified
Safe in the shadow of the Lord
Great is the Lord

Readings

Psalm 127 / Proverbs 9:1-12 / Isaiah 54:11-14 / 1 Corinthians 3:10-17 / Ephesians 2:14-22 / 1 Peter 2:4-10 / Matthew 7:24-27 / 16:13-20 / Luke 20:9-19.

Confession

Lord God, you build your people together as a holy temple, yet we have not been willing to be included in your plan. We have failed to live under your guidance or be moulded by your will. Forgive us, we pray, and help us to stand on the sure foundation of Christ our Lord. Amen.

God our heavenly Father, grant unto you pardon and deliverance from all your wrongdoing and waywardness and restore you to the place he has appointed for you, according to his mighty will in Jesus Christ our Lord. Amen

Prayer

As God joins us together to be a building fit for him, we bring our prayers to him, saying,
Lord, make us one,
And join us together in you.

God of all harmony, your people have long been divided by strife and discord. As Jesus prayed before his death, may all who love you accept your gracious leading and live together in unity.
Lord, make us one,
And join us together in you.

God of all love, your world is torn apart by tension and conflict; violence rules in so many places. As Jesus suffered a criminal's death, may all who live by weapons be won over by your unending love.
Lord, make us one,
And join us together in you.

God of all contentment, so many are unhappy because of illness and fear. As you breathed peace on your disciples, so may the anxious, the unwell and the lonely receive that peace which passes all understanding.

Lord, make us one,
And join us together in you.

God of all hope, this life is but a fleeting shadow, which is gone as quickly as it came. As Jesus' resurrection defeated the powers of evil and death, may all who love and worship you be filled with the joy of your eternal kingdom as they walk with you.

Lord, make us one,
And join us together in you, for the sake of your Son, our Lord Jesus. Amen.

SERMON IDEA

This idea is probably more effective with younger age-groups, and needs some preparation. You'll need a large board covered with felt or baize, a large sheet of card and some velcro with an adhesive back. Cut the card into different shapes (about four or five) making sure you can fit them together into the original shape! Write on each shape one of the 'bricks' in God's church, such as music, teaching, catering, helping. On the reverse place a piece of velcro large enough to stick the shape to the felt.

Talk about each one in turn and explain that on our own we seem to be a funny set of shapes that make no pattern. It's only as we allow God to put us together that we see some kind of pattern. We may find one another easy or difficult, awkward or pleasant, brash or shy. God can use all of us with our various personalities and abilities to build a church made of people who will glorify him. As a final touch you could pin some strips of red felt or ribbon along the joins between the bricks, explaining as you do so that we're held together by the love of God, as demonstrated in the death of his Son.

God's Army

There's a certain overlap here with the Armour of God, and the same caveat applies. Some helpful analogies can be drawn between a human army and God's people, but it must be emphasised that under no circumstances is violence included in our schedule, nor do we have any enemy but the powers of evil. Even when he was arrested Jesus would not allow his disciples to use violence to save him from injustice. However, there are lessons to do with obeying orders, going where we're told, recognising the enemy, and knowing our weak and strong points, which help create an understanding that the Christian faith isn't always a comfortable or easy option, or an escape from everyday pressures and routine. Some modern songs tend to over-emphasise the 'battle' element in the Christian life. This may appeal to some small boys, but it also obscures the truth of the resurrection: that death and evil are already defeated foes. We have only to enter into that victory and claim its power.

HYMNS
Traditional
Onward Christian soldiers
Soldiers of Christ arise
Stand up, stand up, for Jesus
Thy hand O God has guided
Fight the good fight
God of grace and God of glory
Who is on the Lord's side?
All hail the power of Jesus' name
Lift high the Cross
Crown him with many crowns

Modern
In heavenly armour
Rejoice, rejoice!
For this purpose
Victory is on our lips

Show your power O Lord
He that is in us
Be bold, be strong
All hail the Lamb
At your feet we fall
Let God arise

READINGS
Joshua 24:14-18/Psalm 18:30-39/Isaiah 59:15b-21/Ephesians 6:10-20/
2 Timothy 2:1-7/1 Peter 5:6-11/
Matthew 5:43-48/Luke 4:31-37/12:1-7.

CONFESSION
Almighty God, we have failed you by not confronting evil but standing aside. We have not entered into the victory of your Son, but have lost battles by fighting in our own strength. Forgive our self-will and reluctance to trust you, and fill us with the risen life of Christ to fight against sin and evil and enter into your victorious Kingdom, through Christ our Lord. Amen.

May God in his mercy pardon you for all your sins, and fill you with his grace as you fight on the Lord's side. Amen.

PRAYER
We come to the pioneer of our salvation with our thanks and prayers, saying,
Victorious Lord,
Make us faithful in your service.

We thank you for the Cross, the symbol of your triumph over sin and evil. May we keep it in the centre of our vision as we confront wrong in your name.
Victorious Lord,
Make us faithful in your service.

We thank you for the resurrection, the ultimate victory over the powers of darkness. May we enter into it and share your risen life, as our lives

display the marvellous light of your kingdom.
Victorious Lord,
Make us faithful in your service.

We thank you for the ascension, that now you sit for ever in glory at your Father's right hand. May we too become more like you as we seek to serve you wherever you call us,
Victorious Lord,
Make us faithful in your service.

We thank you for your promise to return one day in glory, to right all wrongs and establish your perfect reign for ever. As we look forward in hope may we live to make the world a place more worthy of you.
Victorious Lord,
Make us faithful in your service, so that we may enter into the joy of our Father's Kingdom through our Lord Jesus Christ. Amen.

SERMON IDEA

The more physical and violent aspects of warfare should be minimised, but the concept of an army and how it operates is a helpful picture. The following four points can illustrate some important truths:

1 God's army needs a strategy. We won't get very far if we don't know what we're doing or why we're supposed to do it! A map or diagram of a battleground could be useful here, either on an OHP or a large flip chart. You might even mention a battle that's been won through good strategy. Part of our 'strategy' as Christians is to pray, to read God's Word, and to put our trust in him.

2 No strategy is complete unless we know our enemy. Satan will try to fool us at every stage (he's called the prince of lies!) and we have to recognise that, no matter what the manifestation of evil confronting us, we're really fighting 'principalities and powers'.

3 No battle was ever won without proper equipment. God has given us everything we need to be protected from 'the fiery darts of the evil one' and we need only allow him to deal with the forces of evil when they attack us. Point out that we must never use violence – our weapons are prayer and God's Word. All of this is visually full of impact, whether you use an OHP, a flip-chart, or direct aids such as a sword or a firearm (unloaded!).

4 Most important, an army has to believe in its cause, and believe it will win. Our cause is Jesus and his Kingdom and the victory is already won through his death and resurrection (a simple visual of a cross and empty tomb will be sufficient here).

God's Servants

Although it's most important to stress that God loves us for who we are, not for what we do, the idea that we're God's servants has a significant appeal for our hyperactive society. Children in particular need instructing in how to apply the Christian faith to everyday life. If it has no application it has no relevance either! Action is all very well, but servants also have to be obedient and loyal, qualities not so readily prized .

Serving God is a theme to be found throughout the Bible, always in the context of obedience rather than activity for its own sake, as many of Jesus' parables demonstrate graphically. Mary describes herself as 'God's servant', though all that was required of her was trust. Jesus himself is the supreme servant, the King of all who gave his life for us. He did not come to be served but to serve. God's servants are entrusted with much and are responsible to their Master (cf the parable of the talents, in which it was the attitude rather than the activity which earned commendation or condemnation).

HYMNS
Traditional
Ye servants of God
Strengthen for service, Lord
When I survey
Take my life and let it be
May the mind of Christ my Saviour
Teach me my God and King
True hearted, whole-hearted
Filled with the Spirit's power

Modern
Make me a channel of your peace
When I needed a neighbour
Seek ye first
I want to walk with Jesus Christ
Jesus take me as I am

I want to serve the purpose of God
Send me out from here, Lord
From Heaven you came

READINGS
Joshua 1:1-9/2 Samuel 7:18-29/
Isaiah 42:1-9/Acts 4:23-31/
2 Corinthians 6:3-13/Philippians 2: 1-11/Matthew 25:14-30/Mark 10:32-45/
John 15:18-27.

CONFESSION
Master of all, we acknowledge before you our guilt and shame. We have not been obedient or faithful servants and have failed to fulfil what you have asked of us. We are sorry for not doing what we should have done, and for doing instead what we should not. Forgive us and strengthen us by your Holy Spirit to serve you faithfully and joyfully to the glory of Jesus Christ our Lord. Amen.

Almighty God, who shows mercy to all who come to him in repentance and faith, pardon and deliver you from all your sins and restore you to the presence of him whose service is perfect freedom, Jesus Christ our Lord. Amen.

PRAYER
Our Heavenly Father knows our every need before we ask him. We come to him in confidence, saying,
Heavenly Father,
Strengthen us for your service.

Bless all who serve you in the family of the Church, be they bishops or priests, ordained or lay, poor or rich. May they serve the cause of your Kingdom with loyalty and joy, building up God's people and proclaiming the good news of Jesus.

Master of all,
Strengthen us for your service.

Bless all who serve you in the world,
in national or local government, in
commerce or industry, in authority or
in obedience. May they follow the
paths of righteousness and peace, and
bring your justice to all mankind.
Master of all,
Strengthen us for your service.

Bless all who serve you in humble
ways, unnoticed by the world but
known to you, and obedient to your
will. May they inspire us to do your
will in the common things of life.
Master of all,
Strengthen us for your service.

Bless all who serve you despite pain
and suffering, especially . . . May they
be strengthened in their faith and
patient in their troubles, and know the
joy of your salvation.
Master of all,
Strengthen us for your service.

Bless all whose earthly service has
ended but whose lives continue to bear
fruit to your glory. May we by your
Spirit follow their example and remain
steadfast to your calling until we reach
our heavenly home.
Master of all,
**Strengthen us for your service, and
bring us to your eternal kingdom
where we will hear your 'Well done
good and faithful servant', through
Jesus Christ our Lord. Amen.**

SERMON IDEA
This particular idea is based on Jesus'
parable of the talents and aims to show
that it's our attitude to serving God
that counts with him, not our
competence, because he has promised
to equip us for everything he calls us to
do. You will need three previously
primed volunteers who will be called
up from among the congregation
(fixing is sometimes necessary!). You
should give each of them a task. The
first should have an obviously 'good'
thing to perform, such as cleaning a
chalice, or reading something out – it
has to be easily noticed. The second
should have a job whose end result is
less noticeable, such as polishing a
couple of pews or stacking books. The
third should be given a really menial
task (tidying a corner of the vestry, or
something similarly dirty and unseen).
He should also be primed not to bother
with it! When they go off, talk about
the different ways God might call us to
serve him. On their return reward the
first two, who will have done a good
job, but send the third away with
nothing. Conclude by saying that God
can help us if we're willing to obey
him, but not if we're only interested in
being noticed. All are equal before him,
and have to give account to him of
what they've done.

God's Pilgrims

Considering how frequently it occurs in Scripture we make relatively little of the picture of God's people as pilgrims, on a journey through this life to eternal life. This is a shame as it's just as vibrant and rich as any of the others, and if neglected can lead to an important truth being obscured, namely that the whole of this life must be lived in the light of eternity; that we can never say we've arrived or know it all; and that we are always moving onwards as we journey to our heavenly home.

Our minds easily become earthbound as the pressures and distractions of this life blur our vision of things eternal. It's a great excuse for moving about, or conveying a sense of movement, if the space is too constrained for getting people out of their seats. In some ways this overlaps with All Saints' Day, but it does no harm to reinforce teaching given at other times, and it stands on its own as another description of the Church. If the Church comes across as not static, or even mobile, quite a few will be surprised!

HYMNS

Traditional
Thy hand, O God, has guided
Lead us, Heavenly Father, lead us
Lord of all hopefulness
O Jesus I have promised
Through the night of doubt and sorrow
Guide me, O thou great Jehovah
O happy band of pilgrims
Through all the changing scenes
Children of the heavenly King
O for a closer walk with God

Modern
I want to walk with Jesus Christ
The Spirit lives to set us free
He walked where I walk
We'll walk the land

We shall stand
We are marching
The Lord has led forth his people
Rejoice, rejoice!
Soon, and very soon
Thanks be to God, who gives us

READING

Genesis 28:10-17 / Deuteronomy 2:1-7 / Psalm 107:1-9 / Acts 9:1-19 / Romans 8:18-27 / Hebrews 11:8-16 / Mark 10:46-52 / Luke 14:25-35 / John 11:1-16.

CONFESSION

Heavenly Father you have called us to walk with you and follow your way, yet we have turned aside too easily and allowed you out of our vision. Forgive our waywardness and backsliding, and restore us again to the paths of righteousness for your name's sake. Amen.

God our Father, who forgives all who repent and turn back to him, grant unto you pardon and peace, and bring you back to the path of glory for the sake of his Son Jesus Christ our Lord. Amen.

PRAYER

As we walk, with our heavenly Father, the path of eternal life, we offer him our praise and requests, saying,
Lord of our life,
Accept our prayers.

For all the blessings of this world we give you thanks. You alone are the giver and sustainer of life, and on you we depend for all our needs.
Fill our hearts with gratitude and thankfulness, we pray, and make us mindful of all whose lives do not enjoy what we do.

Lord of our life,
Accept our prayers.

For all whose work enables us to live in
order and comfort we give you thanks.
We pray for governments and
authorities, both national and local,
that their rule may reflect your eternal
kingdom and bring peace and justice to
all people.
Lord of our life,
Accept our prayers.

For all who seek to bring comfort to the
sick and afflicted we give you thanks.
We pray that through their work the
compassion of Jesus may be seen, and
that those who suffer in body or mind
may be healed by his touch.
Lord of our life,
Accept our prayers.

For all who have trod this pilgrim path
before us we give you thanks. May we
faithfully follow in their steps as we
journey through this life to the place
you have prepared for us.
Lord of our life,
**Accept our prayers, and keep us in the
straight way that leads to eternal life.
Amen.**

SERMON IDEA
The basic concept behind this is a
treasure hunt. You'll need to hide some
'treasure' so that it can be found only
by looking at a signpost, looking at a
map and asking someone where to go.
This needs preparation, both in hiding
the 'treasure' and in setting up clues.
Select two or three children and give
them a 'map' to indicate the location of
the treasure. On it mark where they can
find further help from a 'signpost' or a
'helper on the way'. Four or five such

'markers' are probably sufficient, and
you must also make allowances for the
age and ability ranges involved. Point
out that as well as giving us direct
guidance God has given us the Bible,
his Word, as a map for our life. If we
follow it we'll certainly find the
treasure which is God's Kingdom. He
gives us other indications, too, through
prayer or events. It's important at this
juncture not to give the impression that
God writes in large letters in the sky
what his will is – each of us is
responsible for our life, and in offering
it back to God we find he shows us his
perfect and acceptable will. Finally, say
that asking others is a great source of
help on the way, too, and God has
given us one another for such mutual
help and encouragement.

The Body of Christ

The theme of the Church as the Body of Christ has already been covered in part by the Gifts of the Holy Spirit in the section on Pentecost. However, another approach is to use the flexibility of the English language to advantage. The word 'body' can also apply to a group or team of people ('a fine body of men', we might say). Christians aren't always noted for their stunning teamwork, so to convey the idea that God wants us to work together in a co-ordinated way for him is a useful antidote to the impression the Church frequently gives. For most children, these days, teams mean sport, so there are plenty of images available which will appeal. You may need to adjust this to the time of year, or where you are situated (Merseyside would relate to football any time of year!), but the basic points are the same.

HYMNS

Traditional
Blessed be the tie that binds
Help us to help each other, Lord
Christ is the King!
In Christ there is no east or west
Christ, from whom all blessings flow
Glorious things of thee are spoken
All praise to our redeeming Lord
God of grace and God of glory

Modern
For I'm building a people of power
Bind us together
Tell my people I love them
Jesus put this song into our hearts
We'll walk the land
We are a chosen people
Lord make me an instrument
From the sun's rising

READINGS
Genesis 15:1-6/Judges 7:1-21/
Psalm 122/1 Corinthians 12:12-27/
Romans 12:3-8/Colossians 1:9-20/
Matthew 17:14-21/Luke 10:1-12/
John 17:20-26.

CONFESSION
Heavenly Father, you have called us to be one as you are one, but too often we fail to live up to our calling. Forgive us for the times when we damage relationships, fall into conflict, and are unable to work together for your glory. Help us to love one another as you have loved us, that others may see you, the only true God. Amen.

Almighty God, the Father of all mercies, forgive you for all your sins, strengthen you for his service and keep you in eternal life, through Jesus Christ our Lord. Amen.

PRAYER
We pray for the use of God's gifts to his Church, saying,
Jesus, Lord of your Church,
In your mercy hear us.

God our father, you give us gifts that we may work together in the service of your Son. Bless those who lead, that they may be firm in faith, yet humble before you.
Jesus, Lord of your Church,
In your mercy hear us.

Bless those who teach, that they may increase our understanding, and be open to your word for them.
Jesus, Lord of your Church,
In your mercy hear us.

Bless those who minister healing, that they may bring wholeness to others, yet know your healing in themselves.

Jesus, Lord of your Church,
In your mercy hear us.

Bless those through whom you speak,
that they may proclaim your word in
power, yet have their eyes open to your
gentle whisper.
Jesus, Lord of your Church,
In your mercy hear us.

Bless those who work in your world
today, that they may live for you,
fulfil your purposes, and seek your
kingdom first in the complexity of
their daily lives.
Jesus, Lord of your Church,
In your mercy hear us.

Bless those who feel they have no gifts
and are not valued, and those who are
powerless by the world's standards,
that they may share their experience of
the work of your Spirit.
Lord of your Church,
**Hear our prayer, and make us one in
heart and mind to serve you in Christ
our Lord. Amen.**

Adapted from *Church Family Worship*

SERMON IDEA

As a visual aid you could use either
pictures of a well-known sporting team
or, if they're agreeable, one of the
school teams. In either event it's
important to stress the relative roles of
individual skills and the teamwork
which harnesses these skills and makes
them something bigger than the sum of
their parts. A football team is the
chosen example here, but any sport
will do. If you use real players, make
sure they're in the appropriate gear!

In a football team two players stand
out and are noticed – the goalscorer
and the goalkeeper (centre-forward

isn't a term much used these days!).
Point both of these team members out
and, if using living visuals get them to
demonstrate their skills if at all
possible – at least get them to show off
the body movements, even if kicking a
ball might cause damage. They're vital
to a successful football team, but their
skills cannot stand alone. If the
goalkeeper hasn't got a sound defence
in front of him, all his agility won't
save his side. Likewise, the goalscoring
forward needs someone to pass him
the ball. The midfielder who dribbles
the ball brilliantly won't get far if
there's no forward to pick up his
passes, and the defender who tackles
superbly does his work in vain if the
attackers don't take the ball away from
the penalty area. Even modestly gifted
team members who function together
as a team will be more successful than
a bunch of talented individuals all
doing their own thing.

Use this to show that God wants us
to be his 'team' working with one
another to achieve the purposes of his
kingdom. God the Holy Trinity is a
'team' in that sense and we are called
to be like God and reflect his character.
Unlike a football team, however, we
have an extra player, God's Holy Spirit,
who blends us into a cohesive unit for
his glory.